SPELLING ENGLISH

A CONCISE GUIDE TO SPELLING, PUNCTUATION AND STYLE

RONALD S. HORAN

HONEYSETT PRESS

SPELLING ENGLISH

By Ronald S. Horan BA (Hons) Dip Ed MACE
Designed and edited by George Jaksic BA JP

Honeysett Press
First Floor, 1 Renwick Street, Leichhardt NSW 2040 Australia

Typeset in ITC Garamond, Futura and Frutiger fonts and printed by
GeoGraphics Group
PO Box 23, Westgate NSW 2048 Australia

PROUDLY PRINTED IN AUSTRALIA

First printing 1994
9 8 7 6 5 4 3 2 1

National Library of Australia
Cataloguing-in-Publication data:
Horan, R. S. (Ronald Stephen).
Spelling English.

Includes index.
ISBN 0 646 19334 1

1. English language – Orthography and spelling.
2. English language – Punctuation. 3. English language – Style. I. Title.

428.1

Introduction

Spelling English provides a concise yet complete coverage of the rules that operate in the spelling of English. For all the seeming complexity, if you approach the task positively you can by studying the rules improve your spelling. While there are more than a few words that cannot be classified, the rules given cover all the word patterns of the language. *Spelling English* also contains practical guides to those other elements of correct word forms necessary for the formulation of a sentence and also notes on punctuation.

If you earnestly want to write English correctly, there is no short cut. All future attempts to simplify the spelling of English words will, with all certainty, meet the same fate as those unsuccessful efforts made in the past. The genius of the English language does not lend itself to such manipulative devices. So, knowing that there is and will be no easy way, set to the task enthusiastically. Bear in mind that *Spelling English* is organised so as to make your task as simple and as rewarding as possible.

For those whose spelling and knowledge of sentence construction is fairly sound, the book will always serve as a useful and reliable reference. The guidelines given are in keeping with the best general modern practice. Certain other procedures may at times be argued as also being correct, but these in no way invalidate what is presented in the book.

CONTENTS

Page

See Index on pages 91-95 for a detailed listing of the contents.

About the Author

Ron Horan was born in Sydney and had his secondary education at Fort Street Boys High School just before and in the early years of the Second World War. He then entered the Faculty of Arts at The University of Sydney but interrupted his studies to serve in the Royal Australian Air Force for three years. After the war he completed his Bachelor of Arts degree, majoring in French (Honours) and German. He also gained a Diploma in Education. After a short appointment at Sydney Boys High School he joined the staff of Fort Street, where he taught for 36 years. Many of those years were spent as modern languages master and later as deputy principal. His teaching subjects were French, German and English.

Throughout his career, Ron demonstrated great practical concern for correct English spelling, the importance of which is often neglected in schools. As a practical guide for students he compiled the *Fort Street Speller*, which is presented to all pupils upon their arrival at the school. The guide has made its way into many avenues of public administration.

Ron Horan has also been actively involved in the broader sphere of education. He served for ten years as a teacher and deputy principal at the Eastwood Evening College and then for another 22 years as its principal. His contribution to the teaching of foreign languages has been important. With a co-author, he has published French and German course books, which are widely used in Australia and around the world. He has served on many education committees, and was president of the Australian Federation of Modern Language Teachers Associations. He is now education editor for Honeysett Press, maintaining an active role in the study of languages.

Other Publications

A New French Course: Parts 1-5

Senior French: Parts 1-2

A Basic French Vocabulary

A New German Course: Parts 1-2

Everyday German for You (MS.)

The History of the Eastwood Evening College (to 1977)

The Next Seven Years (1977-1983)

Fort Street Speller

Fort Street Songster

Fort Street – The School

In Celebration – Fort Street Old Boys Union Centenary

1 GENERAL SPELLING

1.1 **ie** or **ei**?

With pronunciation as **long e**, **i** comes before **e** except after **c**.
For example

believe	receive
belief	receipt
relieve	perceive
relief	deceive
piece	deceit
niece	ceiling
siege	conceit
chief	conceive
shield	
grief	
wield	
yield	
hygiene	

Exceptions seize, either, neither, counterfeit, protein, caffeine, codeine

Observe also some names of people and places: Neil, Leila, Madeira.

The above general rule "**i** before **e** except after **c**" (the most common in English spelling) covers only the spelling of the **long e** sound. And it covers relatively few words.

Notice the spelling **ei** in words with a **long open a** sound.
For example

eight	vein	neigh
neighbour	sleigh	feign
freight	beige	heinous
weight	rein	deign
skein	veil	inveigh
weigh	reign	inveigle

With the two basic situations for an **ei** spelling in mind, the spelling of all other words with the combination of these two vowels is **ie** except the words listed below.

leisure	foreign	height
heifer	sovereign	sleight *(of hand)*
their	forfeit	seismograph
heir	surfeit	apartheid
heiress	weir	Fahrenheit
heirloom	weird	kaleidoscope

▷

Note The **long e** sound is also spelt other ways. *For example*
sheep, sleep, fleet, deep, steel, meet, peel, heel, reel, feet
heat, leave, teach, clean, steal, meat, peal, heal, real, feat

The **short e** sound is also sometimes spelt **ea**. *For example*
stealth, endeavour, steady, ready, treasure

Note A full exposition of **e** sounds and of all other vowel sounds will be found in the *Tables of Sound and Spelling Patterns*, which begin on *page 15*.

1.2 ise or ize?

Almost all relevant verbs may be spelt with **ise**. *For example*

organise	emphasise
recognise	realise
familiarise	authorise
baptise	standardise
colorise	jeopardise

Except capsize, prize *(cherish)*

Such verbs may also be spelt with **ize** (and always are in American English) except the following.

advertise	compromise	incise
advise	despise	revise
apprise	devise	supervise
chastise	disguise	surmise
circumcise	exercise	surprise
comprise	improvise	televise

Note analyse, paralyse, breathalyse, psychoanalyse

1.3 ce, se; cy, sy

Nouns ending in **ce** or **cy** have their corresponding verbs in **se** or **sy**.

For example

practice *(noun)*	practise *(verb)*
licence *(noun)*	license *(verb)*
device *(noun)*	devise *(verb)*
prophecy *(noun)*	prophesy *(verb)*

Observe a licensed plumber, a practising solicitor – because the adjective is formed from the verb.

Also Only the verb *coerce* ends in **erce**. The few other verbs in the language ending with this sound are spelt **erse**. *For example*

reverse, perverse, obverse, inverse, intersperse

1.4 The letter **l** at the end of a word

Words of one syllable containing a single letter vowel almost always have a **double l**. *For example*

all, well, tell, full, call, fall, will, roll, ill, bill, dull, chill, null, ball, smell, spell, mill, cell, toll, till

Note nil, gel, pal, gal

The **double l** is retained in compounds. *For example*

unwell, refill, recall, downfall, goodwill, foretell, pitfall

But until, enrol, annul

In almost all other cases, the word will end in a **single l**. *For example*

wool, soil, soul, trial, trail, oval, appeal, model, equal, initial, prevail, expel, extol, excel, apparel, parallel

But install

The following four words are spelt with a **single final l**, except in American English where a *double l* occurs.

enrol, fulfil, instil, appal

To remember the main point, bear in mind the words *till* and *until*.

1.5 **ant** or **ent** (**ance** or **ence**)?

Adjectives ending in **ant** or **ent** have their corresponding nouns in **ance** or **ence** respectively There is no rule however for whether the adjective ends in **ant** or **ent**. *For example*

tolerant	tolerance
reluctant	reluctance
observant	observance
abundant	abundance
vigilant	vigilance
resistant	resistance
relevant	relevance
arrogant	arrogance
elegant	elegance
significant	significance
extravagant	extravagance
repentant	repentance

▷

existent	existence
permanent	permanence
negligent	negligence
independent	independence
insistent	insistence
prevalent	prevalence
coherent	coherence
indulgent	indulgence
persistent	persistence
expedient	expedience
transcendent	transcendence

Note The word *dependent* is an adjective.
The word *dependant* is a noun referring to a person.
The abstract noun is *dependence.*

Also defence, defensive; offence, offensive

There are also nouns in **ance** and **ence** that have no corresponding adjective ending in **nt**. No rule governs the noun ending.

For example

acceptance	occurrence
ambulance	preference
remembrance	deference
maintenance	pestilence
perseverance	precedence
conveyance	experience

Note allegiance

There are very few words in **ense**. The common ones are the following.

condense	incense	recompense
dense	intense	sense
dispense	license *(verb)*	suspense
expense	nonsense	tense
immense		

Note licence *(noun)*

1.6 **able** or **ible**?

There is likewise no rule for whether the adjective ends in **able** or **ible**.

For example

advisable	audible
respectable	responsible
dependable	eligible
excitable	negligible

acceptable	susceptible
applicable	feasible
irreplaceable	contemptible
preferable	accessible
memorable	infallible
movable	plausible
irritable	compatible
unforgettable	corruptible
manageable	convertible
irrevocable	irresistible
indispensable	irrepressible
available	irreversible

1.7 **eous** or **ious**?

There is similarly no rule for whether the adjective ends in **eous** or **ious**.

For example

hideous	laborious
spontaneous	notorious
courteous	oblivious
bounteous	illustrious
homogeneous	abstemious
instantaneous	copious
extraneous	spurious
discourteous	tedious
miscellaneous	infectious
simultaneous	conscientious
nauseous	pretentious
righteous	malicious
gorgeous	atrocious
courageous	pernicious
outrageous	contagious
advantageous	religious

1.8 **ery**, **ary** or **ory**?

Almost all words ending in **ery** are nouns. *For example*

stationery, bribery, treachery, drudgery, forgery, cemetery, monastery, effrontery, surgery, artillery

Except Adjectives formed mostly by adding **y** to a noun ending in **er**.

For example

blustery, splintery, blistery; slippery ▷

Both nouns and adjectives end in **ary**. *For example*

dictionary	necessary
boundary	imaginary
burglary	supplementary
glossary	stationary
vocabulary	honorary
tributary	voluntary
granary	contemporary
missionary	auxiliary

Both nouns and adjectives end in **ory**. *For example*

directory	satisfactory
inventory	compulsory
laboratory	introductory
factory	preparatory
promontory	congratulatory
oratory	exploratory
purgatory	derogatory
offertory	conciliatory

Note injury, perjury

1.9 **er** or **or**?

Nouns ending in **er**, mostly formed from verbs, indicate the *doer* or *maker*. However, some nouns with this indication end in **or**. *For example*

singer	actor
writer	impostor
baker	cultivator
prowler	impersonator
jeweller	malefactor
milliner	narrator
controller	predator
importer	contractor
petitioner	counsellor
pensioner	operator

Some few words permit both forms for the *doer*. *For example*

adviser, advisor; convener, convenor

Some few words have both forms, the **er** form being a person who does the action, and the form in **or** a thing serving a technical purpose. At times only the second form exists. *For example*

adapter, conveyer
adaptor, conveyor, resistor, calculator, accelerator, generator

But computer, propeller, receiver, transmitter, soap-saver

Some *doer* words are spelt with **ar** as are other words. *For example*

scholar, liar, registrar, beggar
grammar, calendar, nectar, hangar, altar, cellar

1.10 **or** or **our**?

Apart from *doer* words, most words with the relevant sound end in **our**.

For example

colour	glamour	humour
neighbour	valour	rumour
vigour	savour	favour
honour	endeavour	harbour

Note behaviour, saviour

The following end in **or**

terror	horror	tremor
error	squalor	stupor
tenor	pallor	torpor

Note languor; anchor, liquor, mirror, razor

1.11 **city** or **sity**?

The letter **c** or **s** can in most words be traced to a corresponding adjective or verb. *For example*

authentic	authenticity
eccentric	eccentricity
complicate	complicity
reciprocate	reciprocity
perverse	perversity
diverse	diversity
pompous	pomposity
generous	generosity
impetuous	impetuosity
verbose	verbosity

Note

simplicity	propensity
velocity	animosity
paucity	

1.12 **cial** or **tial**?

If the letter **t** is found in a corresponding base word, the spelling is **tial**. If however the base word has the letter **c**, the spelling may be either **cial** or **tial**. *For example*

partial		official
impartial		racial
torrential		provincial
potential		artificial
presidential		prejudicial
	But	circumstantial
		essential
		influential
		preferential

1.13 **acy** or **asy**?

The **acy** ending is by far the more common. *For example*

democracy	accuracy
privacy	delicacy
fallacy	pharmacy
intimacy	supremacy

The only common **asy** words are the following:

ecstasy, fantasy, idiosyncrasy

Note	prophecy	courtesy
	secrecy	heresy
	policy	hypocrisy
		pleurisy
		leprosy

1.14 **ction** or **xion**? *(See also 1.15)*

Most words with a **k** sound are spelt **ction**. *For example*

reflection	action	collection
connection	correction	introduction
inflection	fraction	satisfaction
deflection	friction	predilection
	erection	construction
	conviction	direction
	section	protection
	production	inspection

The words in the first column have an optional spelling in **xion**.

A few words only must be written with **xion**: complexion, crucifixion.

1.15 **tion**, **sion** or **cion**?

Apart from the words in *Section 1.14*, there is the further problem of words that end in **tion** (not preceded by *c*) or in **sion** or **cion**.

Only two common words end in **cion**: suspicion, coercion.

As for **tion** and **sion**, perhaps a look at the various types of words will be the best aid. *For example*

position	deception	exertion
addition	reception	extortion
solution	suggestion	contention
notion	option	intention
decision	expulsion	diversion
persuasion	ascension	tension
confusion	aversion	dimension
incision	extension	aspersion

Words with a **z** sound are all spelt **sion**.

Observe also words ending in **ssion**. *For example*

admission, permission, possession, discussion, fission, obsession

Note fashion, cushion

Notice also that many nouns indicating persons end in **cian**. *For example*

musician, politician, technician, mathematician

1.16 **ch** or **tch**?

After a consonant **ch** is the spelling. *For example*

church	branch	search
lurch	arch	squelch

After a vowel consisting of more than one letter **ch** is the spelling.

For example

teach	approach	screech
touch	brooch	couch

After a vowel consisting of a single letter **tch** is the spelling. *For example*

catch	fetch	scratch
match	hutch	hatch
watch	witch	hitch

▷

But some common words are exceptions. *For example*

such	spinach	attach
much	sandwich	detach
which	ostrich	rich

1.17 **cede**, **ceed** or **sede**?

The words *proceed*, *succeed* and *exceed* are the only verbs of more than one syllable with **c** and the **long e** and **d** sound at the end to be spelt with **ceed**. All the others end in **cede** except *supersede*.

For example

precede, recede, intercede, concede, accede, secede

Note procedure

1.18 **efy** or **ify**?

The only verbs to end in **efy** are *putrefy*, *rarefy*, *stupefy* and *liquefy*. All others of similar sound end in **ify**. *For example*

terrify	villify	falsify	purify
horrify	glorify	mystify	fortify
verify	classify	notify	certify
indemnify	identify	simplify	petrify
nullify	exemplify	solidify	specify

1.19 **y** or **ie**?

Most words ending in the **short i** sound are spelt with a **y**.
For example

silly	marry	worry	hurry
carry	angry	happy	lorry

Some shortened forms and diminutives are spelt with **ie**. *For example*

movie	budgie	goalie	walkie-talkie
oldie	bookie	cookie	bikie
laddie	girlie	chappie	cutie
lassie	bickie	cossie	sickie
swaggie	(bikkie)	(cozzie)	Aussie

Except buddy, dolly, pussy

And with some words the **ie** spelling is preferred although **y** is correct.
For example

caddie	caddy	hippie	hippy
junkie	junky	softie	softy
rookie	rooky	cabbie	cabby
doggie	doggy	nightie	nighty
goodie	goody	baddie	baddy

1.20 **ae** or **e**?

Some words are spelt with an **ae** in which the **a** is sometimes omitted.
For example

mediaeval, aesthetic, encyclopaedia, anaemia, haemoglobin, haemorrhage, leukaemia, archaeology, paediatric, orthopaedic

While today the word *medieval* is usually spelt without the **a**, standard practice is to retain it in all others.

Tables of Sound and Spelling Patterns – Vowels

The function of the following tables is to serve as a guide to the spelling and the sound. The arrangement is according to sound, showing the spelling for that sound. The table can thus be used from spelling to sound and from sound to spelling. The words given are merely examples.

When only one or two common words constitute a sub-group, no notation appears in the general tables. See the listing of unusual pronunciations for the spelling beneath the **i** table on *page 19*.

The patterns do not show the indeterminate vowel sounds of English at the beginning and ending of words in speech at normal speed. In modern English these sounds tend to become indistinguishable from one another in any case. Nor do the patterns take account of any change brought about by the occurrence of vowels in unstressed syllables. Account is further not taken of vowels that have an unusual vowel pattern borrowed from another language. The vowels of borrowed words and of many proper nouns are not indicated. The patterns are concerned with the basic words of the language.

The behaviour of the letter **r** in modern English is to be noted in regard to vowels. In a word having **r** as its final letter preceded by a vowel, the **r** is fully pronounced only before a following vowel sound.

Slight differences in pronunciation between that of Britain and Australia (and other English-speaking countries) have to be appreciated when consulting a dictionary. This also applies in the case of certain borrowed words. Indication is not given of cases where a word has two (or more) accepted pronunciations.

Sound Symbols used in the Spelling Tables

The symbols are arranged for the easiest reference.	**ă** (hat)	**ĕ** (yes)	**ĭ** (bit)	**ŏ** (not)	**ŭ** (hut)
				o͝o (book)	
The word in brackets here denotes the vowel sound.	**ā** (name)	**ē** (scene)	**ī** (bite)	**ō** (note)	**ū** (use)
The spelling patterns show the variations in the pronunciation of the English vowels. They will serve as a guide to the pronunciation of each word.				**o͞o** (boot)	
	ār (farm)	**ēr** (beer)	**īr** (fire)	**oor** (poor)	**ūr** (pure)
	âr (bare)	**êr** (verb)	**îr** (bird)	**ôr** (port)	**ûr** (surf)
		= îr			
		= ûr			
	ah (bath)				
	aw (law)			**ow** (cow)	
				owr (sour)	
				oi (boil)	

Note The sound symbol **âr** really denotes an e sound.

The sound symbol **aw** really denotes an o sound.

The sound symbol **o͞o** really denotes a **u** sound.

Note A final **-e** after a single consonant usually has the effect of lengthening the vowel in the preceding syllable: name, scene, bite, note, use.

sound	*spelling*	
ȧ	a	hat, bad, gather, tact; have
ā	a-e	name, gaze, lane, safe
	a	agent, naked, paling, change
	ai	aid, fail, train, praise
	ay	say, pay, relay, payment
	ea	great, break, steak
	ei	vein, rein, feint, heinous
	eig	reign, deign
	eigh	weigh, eight, eighth, freight
	ey	grey, obey, they, convey
ār	ar	farm, charge, car, garlic; are
	ear	heart, hearth
âr	are	bare, glare, square, dare
	aer	aeroplane, aerial, aerospace, aerated
	air	air, fair, pair, despair, lair
	ear	bear, wear, pear
	eir	their, heir, heirloom
	ere	there, where
ah	a	bath, draft, castle, pass
	al	calm, palm, balm, qualm
	au (+gh = f)	laugh, draught
aw	aw	law, paw, dawn, drawl
	a	water, also, wall, called
	al	talk, walk
	au	haul, maul, pause, taut
	augh	taught, caught, haughty
	ough (+t)	ought, bought, thought, fought
Also		
ĕ	a	any, many, says
	ea	bread, deaf, heaven, weapon
ē	ae	aegis, encyclopaedia, haemoglobin
	ea	bean, east, teak, eager
ēr	ear	fear, spear, beard, appear
êr	ear	earth, heard, early, rehearse
ŏ	a	what, was, squad, squander
	au	sausage, Australia, cauliflower
ō	oa	oat, boat, coast, hoax, goal
ôr	ar	war, warm, dwarf, towards
	oar	board, oar, roar, hoarse

e

sound	*spelling*	
ĕ	e	yes, bell, send, elbow, gentle
	ea	bread, deaf, heaven, weapon
	ei	leisure, heifer
	eo	leopard, jeopardy
	a	any, many, says
ē	e-e	scene, these, theme, eve
	e	she, equal, gardenia, regal
	ee	feet, meet, seek, agree
	ie	piece, chief, yield, belief
	ei	ceiling, receive, deceive, conceit
	ea	bean, east, teak, eager
	ae	aegis, encyclopaedia, haemoglobin
	i	police, ravine, machine
	oe	foetus, amoeba, phoenix
ēr	eer	beer, queer, career, mutineer
	ear	fear, spear, beard, appear
	eir	weir, weird
	er	hero, zero, query; here
	ier	pier, tier, pierce, bier
êr	er	verb, her, nerve, verve; were
	ear	earth, heard, early, rehearse
	or	word, worm, worse
	our	courtesy, journey
îr = êr	ir	bird, birth, dirty, thirst
ûr = êr	ur	surf, blur, church, occur
Also		
ā	ea	great, break, steak
	ei	vein, rein, feint, heinous
	eig	reign, deign
	eigh	weigh, eight, eighth, freight
	ey	grey, obey, they, convey
ār	ear	heart, hearth
âr	aer	aeroplane, aerial, aerospace, aerated
	are	bare, glare, square, dare
	ear	bear, wear, pear
	eir	their, heir, heirloom
	ere	there, where
ĭ	ei	foreign, sovereign
	ey	valley, monkey, donkey
ī	ei(gh)	Fahrenheit, seismograph, height
	ie	lie, die, belie, tried
ō	oe	toe, foe, hoe, doe
o͞o	ew	chew, drew, threw, jewel
	oe	shoe, canoe
	ue	true, blue, glue, rue
ū	eu	feud, Europe, pneumonia
	ew / iew	few, new, dew, pew / view, review
	ue	due, cue, hue, ensue

sound	*spelling*	
ĭ	i	bit, drill, fish; give
	y	gymnast, rhythm, hymn, lorry
	ei	foreign, sovereign
	ey	valley, monkey, donkey
ī	i-e	bite, size, fine, pile
	i	trial, kind, wild, pliers
	ie	lie, die, belie, tried
	igh	high, sigh, night, tight
	ei(gh)	Fahrenheit, seismograph, height
	y	sky, rely, hyena; dye
	uy	buy, guy
īr	ire	fire, hire, acquire, require
	ier	fiery, hierarchy, hieroglyphics
	yre	tyre, lyre, pyre
îr = êr	ir	bird, birth, dirty, thirst
Also		
ā	ai	aid, fail, train, praise
	ei	vein, rein, feint, heinous
	eig	reign, deign
	eigh	weigh, eight, eighth, freight
ār	air	air, fair, pair, despair, lair
	eir	their, heir, heirloom
ĕ	ei	leisure, heifer
ē	ei	ceiling, receive, deceive, conceit
	i	police, ravine, machine
	ie	piece, chief, yield, belief
ēr	eir	weir, weird
	ier	pier, tier, pierce, bier
o͞o	ui	fruit, cruise, bruise, juice
oi	oi	boil, oil, devoid, poignant
	oy/uoy	boy, toy, enjoy, enjoyment / buoy

Unusual Pronunciations

ā	gaol	ēr	souvenir	ō	sew
ā	gauge	êr	chauffeur	ō	brooch
ā	café, fiancée	êr	colonel	ō	mauve
ār	clerk, sergeant			ō	yeoman
ār	bazaar	ĭ	English	o͞o	rheumatism
aw	broad, broadcast	ĭ	women	o͞o	manoeuvre
ĕ	said	ĭ	busy, business	oor	tour
ĕ	friend	ĭ	build	oor	pleuresy
ĕ	bury	ĭ	sieve		
ĕ	aesthetic	ī	aisle	ŭ	does
ē	people			ŭ	blood
ē	key	o͝o	woman	ū	beauty
ē	quay	o͝o	wolf	ū	nuisance

sound	spelling	
ŏ	o	not, doll, wrong, olive
	ou (+ gh = f)	cough, trough
	a	what, squad, was, squander
	au	sausage, Australia, cauliflower
o͝o	oo	book, look, brook, rookie
	ou	would, could, should
	u	put, push, butcher, full
ō	o-e	note, hole, wrote, rove
	o	no, most, bold, over, omen
	oe	toe, foe, hoe, doe
	oa	oat, boat, coast, hoax, goal
	ol	folk, yolk
	ou	mould, shoulder
	ough	though, dough, furlough
	ow	low, slow, bowl, flown; owe
o͞o	oo	boot, loose, choose, pool, too
	o	do, to; lose, move
	oe	shoe, canoe
	ou	you, soup, group, youth
	ough	through
	ew	chew, drew, threw, jewel
	u	rude, rule, ruby, truth
	ue	true, blue, glue, rue
	ui	fruit, cruise, bruise, juice
	uo	fluorescent, fluoride
oor	oor	poor, moor
	ure	sure, assure, ensure, insure
ôr	or	port, force, absorb, forty, shore
	oor	door, floor
	oar	board, oar, roar, hoarse
	our	four, course, pour, your
	ar	war, warm, dwarf, towards
ow	ow	cow, brow, down, endow
	ou	out, doubt, mouth, scrounge
	ough	bough, drought, plough
owr	our	sour, flour, our, hour
oi	oi	boil, oil, devoid, poignant
	oy/uoy	boy, toy, enjoy, enjoyment; buoy
Also		
aw	aw	law, paw, dawn, drawl
	ough (+t)	ought, bought, thought, fought
ĕ	eo	leopard, jeopardy
ē	oe	foetus, amoeba, phoenix
êr	or	word, worm, worse
	our	courtesy, journey
ŭ	o	honey, mother, tongue; love, come, done
	ou	touch, nourish, couple
	ou (+ gh = f)	tough, rough, enough

U

sound	*spelling*	
ŭ	u	hut, bump, such, lunch
	ou	touch, nourish, couple
	ou (+ gh = f)	tough, rough, enough
	o	honey, mother, tongue; love, come, done
ū	u-e	use, huge, astute, resume
	u	human, bugle, numeral, putrid
	ue	due, cue, hue, ensue
	eu	feud, Europe, pneumonia
	ew	few, new, dew, pew
	iew	view, review
ūr	ure	pure, cure, endure, allure
ûr = êr	ur	surf, blur, church, occur
Also		
au	au (+ gh = f)	laugh, draught
aw	au	haul, maul, pause, taut
	augh	taught, caught, naughty
	ough (+t)	ought, bought, thought, fought
êr	our	courtesy, journey
ī	uy	buy, guy
ŏ	au	sausage, Australia, cauliflower
	ou (+ gh = f)	cough, trough
o͝o	u	put, push, butcher, full
ō	ou	would, could, should
	ou	mould, shoulder
	ough	though, dough, furlough
o͞o	u	rude, rule, ruby, truth
	ue	true, blue, glue, rue
	ui	fruit, cruise, bruise, juice
	uo	fluorescent, fluoride
	ou	you, soup, group, youth
	ough	through
	ew	chew, drew, threw, jewel
oor	ure	sure, assure, ensure, insure
ôr	our	four, course, pour, your
ow	ou	out, doubt, mouth, scrounge
	ough	bough, drought, plough
owr	our	sour, flour, our, hour

Note the use of **u** to harden the **g** before **e** and **i** as in:
guess, guest
guilt, guild, guitar
guide, guile, disguise

Also guard, guarantee

And also the use of **u** sounded as **w** after **s**, **g** and **q** as in:
persuade, suede, suave; language, languish; square, quit

2 PREFIXES

2.1 **ante** or **anti**?

The prefix **ante** means *before*. *For example*

antechamber	antenatal
antediluvian	antecedent

The prefix **anti** means *against* or *opposite*. *For example*

anti-aircraft	anticlimax
antibiotic	antidote
antipathy	anti-intellectual
antisocial	anti-hero
anti-Semitic	antithesis
antiseptic	anticlockwise
antitoxin	anti-American

Exception anticipate

Note No hyphen is generally used except before a vowel or a capital letter.

2.2 **fore** or **for**?

Words beginning with **fore** have the meaning *before* or *in front*. *For example*

foreword	foreshore	foreboding
forecourt	foresee	forewarn
foresight	forecast	foreman
foretell	forehead	forefinger
foreground	forestall	foreshadow

If the *before* or *in front* idea is not part of the word, the spelling is **for**. *For example*

forgive	forbid	format
fortuitous	formula	forfeit
formation	forget	fortunate
forlorn	formidable	forsake

Note foreclose; forward
forgather *or* foregather

Also forebear *and/or* forbear
forgo *and/or* forego

2.3 Loss of one **l**

Monosyllables (words of one syllable) ending in **double l** usually have one **l** omitted when they are prefixed to another word beginning with a consonant. *For example*

all	already
all	altogether
well	welcome
well	welfare
chill	chilblain

Note all right

2.4 **il**, **im**, **in**, **ir**

These prefixes have the meaning *not* and also the meaning *in* or *on*. Apart from the **n** words, words with these meanings have a **double l**, **m** or **r**. The **n** words are the only real problem. There is a **double n** only when the prefix is placed in front of a word beginning with **n**. There are very few words with **inn**, the common ones being listed below. *For example*

legal	–	illegal	illuminate
literate	–	illiterate	illusion
mortal	–	immortal	illustrate
migration	–	immigration	immaculate
relevant	–	irrelevant	irrigate
responsible	–	irresponsible	irritate
resistible	–	irresistible	immense
audible	–	inaudible	inane
accurate	–	inaccurate	inoculate
exact	–	inexact	ineffable
equitable	–	inequitable	inertia
imitable	–	inimitable	initiate
offensive	–	inoffensive	inundate
			innocent
			innocuous
			innate
			innumerable
			innovation
			innuendo

2.5 **dis** and **mis**

When the prefixes **dis** and **mis** begin a word, a **double s** occurs only when the prefix stands in front of a word beginning with **s**. Sometimes the base word is a Latin word. The two prefixes have a range of meaning, usually with a negative function. *For example*

disappear	dissimilar
disrepute	dissolve
discharge	dissatisfy
disapprove	dissuade
disengage	dissent
discourage	dissipate
mislead	misspell
mishap	misshapen
mistime	misstate
mistake	misspent

2.6 **ex**(**h**)

The words *exhale*, *exhaust*, *exhibit*, *exhilarate*, *exhort*, *exhume* and their derivatives are the only words in which **ex** is followed by **h**. In other words beginning with **ex** (with a variety of function) no *h* is found.

For example

exalt	exonerate	exegesis
exert	exorbitant	exasperate
exotic	exuberant	exaggerate
exult	exorcism	exacerbate
exude	exemplify	exemplary

---

3 SUFFIXES

3.1 Words ending in a mute (silent) **e** retain the **e** when a suffix beginning with a consonant is added and omit the **e** when followed by a suffix beginning with a vowel. *For example*

love	loving	lovable	lovely
note	noted	noting	notable
inflate	inflated	inflating	inflatable
pursue	pursued	pursuing	pursuer
challenge	challenged	challenging	
come	coming	comely	
lustre	lustrous		
shame	shameful	shameless	
awe	awesome	awestruck	
large	larger	largest	
ache	ached	aching	
glue	glued	gluing	
queue	queued	queuing	
taste	tasteless	tasty	

But there are a few exceptions. *For example*

argue	argument
awe	awful
true	truly
due	duly
whole	wholly
nine	ninth
eerie	eerily
blame	blameable
acre	acreage
mile	mileage
whinge	whingeing
singe	singeing

To keep the **c** and **g** soft, words ending in **ce** or **ge** retain the **e** before adding the suffixes **able** and **ous**. *For example*

change	changeable	changing
courage	courageous	encouraging
notice	noticeable	noticing
knowledge	knowledgeable	acknowledging

3.2 When a suffix beginning with a vowel is added to a monosyllable (one-syllable word) ending with a single consonant preceded by a single vowel, the consonant is **doubled**. *For example*

sad	sadder	saddest
hug	hugging	hugged
big	bigger	biggest
bar	barred	barring
fit	fitted	fitting
quiz	quizzed	quizzing

But	fool	fooled	foolery
	beam	beamed	beaming

Observe the following pairs.

scar	scarred	scare	scared
star	starred	stare	stared
bar	barred	bare	bared

Observe that the letters **w**, **x** and **y** never occur doubled.

bow	bowed	bowing
mix	mixed	mixing
box	boxed	boxing
toy	toyed	toying

3.3 When a suffix beginning with a vowel is added to a word of more than one syllable ending with a single consonant preceded by a single vowel, the consonant is doubled **if the accent is on the final syllable**.

For example

infer	inferred	inferring
omit	omitted	omitting
commit	committed	committal
refer	referred	referral
begin	beginner	beginning
occur	occurred	occurrence
prefer	preferred	preferring
transfer	transferred	transferring
confer	conferred	conferring
regret	regretted	regrettable
forget	forgetting	forgettable

As against

offer	offered	offering
suffer	suffered	suffering
gallop	galloped	galloping

	happen	happened	happening
	benefit	benefited	benefiting
	visit	visited	visitor
	interpret	interpreted	interpreter
	profit	profited	profitable
And	maintain	maintained	maintenance
	appear	appeared	appearance
	proclaim	proclaimed	proclaiming
	condemn	condemned	condemning

Remember the letters **w**, **x** and **y**.

allow	allowed	allowance
relax	relaxing	relaxed
enjoy	enjoyed	enjoyable

Note that the consonant does not double if the accent on the word is changed by the addition: reference, referee, preference, preferable, conference, inference, etc.

Note transferable

The question of doubling or not doubling a single consonant when an ending is added is the most vexing element of English spelling. Apart from the few exceptions noted below, the rules are basically simple covering all words no matter of how many syllables. Note the four essentials for doubling.

Provided that the suffix begins with a vowel, a final consonant doubles if it is single, if it is preceded by a single vowel and if the accent is on the final syllable.

If any one of the four conditions is not met, then the consonant is not doubled.

Observations concerning exceptions

A Words ending in a **single l** preceded by a single vowel generally double the **l** before a suffix beginning with a vowel irrespective of where the accent falls. *For example*

appal	appalling	appalled
travel	traveller	travelling
excel	excelled	excellence
extol	extolled	extolling
rival	rivalled	unrivalled
jewel	jeweller	jewellery
propel	propelled	propeller
cancel	cancelled	cancelling
marvel	marvelling	marvellous

▷

But	assail	assailed	assailant
	appeal	appealing	appealed

Exceptions unparalleled; woollen, woolly; dialling, dialled

And some adjectives ending in **ous**. *For example*

miraculous, perilous, ridiculous, scandalous

And generally when the suffix is **ity**, **ist**, **ism** or **ise**/**ize**. *For example*

	prodigal	prodigality
	frugal	frugality
	equal	equality
	special	specialist
	final	finalist
	fatal	fatalism
	civil	civilise
	equal	equalise
But	tranquil	tranquillity
	medal	medallist
	panel	panellist
	crystal	crystallise

B Words ending in **ic** add **k** before a suffix beginning with **e**, **i** or **y** to preserve the **k** sound. *For example*

picnic	picnicker	picnicking
frolic	frolicking	frolicsome
panic	panicked	panicky
mimic	mimicking	mimicry
traffic	trafficking	trafficker

Note trafficator

C *Notice* these exceptions ending in **p**.

worship	worshipped	worshipping
kidnap	kidnapped	kidnapper
handicap	handicapped	handicapper

D *Notice also* compound verbs and words that behave as compounds. *For example*

horsewhip	horsewhipped	horsewhipping
eavesdrop	eavesdropped	eavesdropping
zigzag	zigzagged	zigzagging
hobnob	hobnobbed	hobnobbing

3.4 Nouns ending in **our** omit the **u** when the suffixes **ous**, **ious**, **ation**, **ise** (or **ize**), **ary**, **ial**, **ific**, **iferous**, are added. The **u** is retained with most other suffixes. *For example*

honour	honourable	honorary	honorific
colour	colorise	colouring	colorant
humour	humorous	humourless	humorist
vigour	vigorous	invigoration	invigorating
labour	laborious	labourer	labouring
armour	armoury	armorial	
odour	odorous	odoriferous	deodorant

3.5 Words ending in **y** preceded by a consonant change the **y** to **i** before all suffixes except **ing**. Notice that **es** is added in relevant present tense forms (not just *s* as in other verbs) and **ed** in the past forms. *For example*

cry	cries	cried	crying
defy	defies	defiance	defying
tidy	tidier	tidying	tidiest
glory	glorify	glorious	glorification
carry	carrying	carrier	carried
dry	driest	drily *(or dryly)*	drier
beauty	beautiful	beautify	beautician

Except beauteous, bounteous, miscellaneous
wryly, spryly; shyness, dryness, slyness, etc.
fortyish, fiftyish, etc.

Observe In words ending in **y** preceded by a vowel, the **y** does not usually change.

But paid, repaid, laid, said, daily, gaily, gaiety

3.6 Verbs ending in **ie** change this to **y** before **ing**. *For example*

die	dying	tie	tying
lie	lying	vie	vying

Words ending in **ee**, **oe**, **ye**, retain the final **e** before all suffixes except those beginning with **e**. *For example*

see	seeing	foreseeable	
agree	agreeing	agreed	agreeable
canoe	canoeing		
dye	dyeing	dyed	

Note roneo – roneoed, roneoing; lasso – lassoed, lassoing

3.7 **y** as a suffix

In the case of adjectives formed by the addition of **y**, most follow the general rule for suffixes. *For example*

shadow	shadowy	soot	sooty
noise	noisy	run	runny
bone	bony	grit	gritty
poke	poky	panic	panicky
smoke	smoky	gravel	gravelly
wire	wiry	chill	chilly

But in some cases the **e** is retained. *For example*

price	pricey	dice	dicey
mate	matey	glue	gluey

Note fiery; clayey, gooey

3.8 When the word **full** is to be added to the end of a word, one **l** is lost. *For example*

shameful	handful	forgetful
hopeful	useful	spoonful
sinful	cupful	thoughtful

3.9 Before a suffix beginning with a consonant, a word ending in **double l** usually has one **l** omitted. *For example*

install	instalment	spell	spelt
skill	skilful	smell	smelt
will	wilful	spill	spilt
full	fully		

Note illness, stillness, etc.

And fulfil

3.10 To form an adverb, add **ly** to the adjective, except in the case of adjectives ending in **ll** when only a **y** is added. An **e** preceded by **l** and one or more consonants will fall away and only **y** will be added. A final **y** preceded by a consonant becomes an **i**. An adjective ending in **ly** (such as *lovely, gentlemanly*) does not normally form an adverb.

For example

quickly	slowly	vastly	jokingly
rarely	scarcely	solely	definitely
coolly	evilly	locally	beautifully
fully	dully	shrilly	
simply	amply	idly	probably
easily	readily	warily	shabbily
slily	shily	drily	

Note wholly, truly, duly
daily, gaily; coyly; eerily

And The words *shy*, *sly* and *dry* also have *shyly*, *slyly* and *dryly*.
The words *wry* and *spry* have only *wryly* and *spryly*.

Adjectives ending with **ic** usually add **ally** to form adverbs. *For example*

basically, eccentrically, historically, economically, optimistically

But publicly, politicly *(sensibly)*

3.11 Endings of words

The endings illustrated in the following sets do not for the most part constitute suffixes. The sets of endings demand attention because of the similarity of pronunciation but with differing spelling.

A (i) metal, total, lethal, mental; bridal, central, global
(ii) tassel, mussel, vessel, kernel, funnel
(iii) muscle, bridle, gamble, trestle, mettle, hassle, tussle, gristle
(iv) lentil, fossil, weevil, basil
(v) gambol

B (i) luggage, beverage, heritage, mortgage, cartage, cartilage
(ii) marriage, carriage
(iii) knowledge, acknowledge
(iv) privilege, sacrilege, college
(v) porridge

C (i) lethargy
(ii) strategy
(iii) energy, allergy
(iv) prodigy
(v) apology, physiology, meteorology, genealogy
(vi) liturgy

4 PLURAL OF NOUNS

The spelling of the plural of the noun in English provides overall little problem. The plurals are for the most part spelt as they are pronounced, the only difficulty being in the case of words ending in **o** and a few of foreign extraction. The rules for the forming of the plural are given here.

4.1 Most nouns add **s** to the singular to form the plural. *For example*

book	books
noun	nouns
answer	answers
question	questions
word	words
brother	brothers
name	names
horse	horses
facsimile	facsimiles
liaison	liaisons
taxi	taxis
alibi	alibis
replica	replicas
gnu	gnus

the Smiths
the Wests
the Nguyens
the McKibbons

4.2 Nouns ending in **s**, **x**, **z**, **sh** or **ch** (pronounced *ch*) form their plural by adding **es**. *For example*

box	boxes
gas	gases
business	businesses
ash	ashes
church	churches
waltz	waltzes
bus	buses
fox	foxes
cross	crosses
branch	branches
bush	bushes
lens	lenses
summons	summonses

the Joneses
the Foxes
the Rosses
the MacIntoshes

Note stomach (stomachs)
quiz (quizzes)

Sometimes a proper noun ending in **s** suffers no change. *For example*

the Geddes
the Jennings

4.3 Nouns ending in **fe** or **lf**, and some ending in **f**, form their plural by changing the **f** into **v** before adding **es**. *For example*

knife	knives	thief	thieves
life	lives	leaf	leaves
wife	wives	loaf	loaves
shelf	shelves	sheaf	sheaves
wolf	wolves		
half	halves		

Other words ending in **f**, including those ending in **ff**, form their plural simply by adding **s**. *For example*

roof	roofs	waif	waifs
chief	chiefs	dwarf	dwarfs
proof	proofs	cliff	cliffs
chef	chefs	cuff	cuffs

The following permit both plurals.

wharf	wharves, wharfs
scarf	scarfs, scarves
hoof	hoofs, hooves
handkerchief	handkerchiefs, handkerchieves

4.4 Nouns ending in **y** preceded by a vowel add **s** to form the plural, but nouns ending in **y** preceded by a consonant change the **y** to **i** and add **es**. *For example*

boy	boys
play	plays
day	days
essay	essays
alloy	alloys
tray	trays
valley	valleys
monkey	monkeys
take-away	take-aways

▷

copy	copies
story	stories
cry	cries
sky	skies
hobby	hobbies
city	cities
trophy	trophies
lady	ladies
folly	follies
lolly	lollies
industry	industries

Note	lay-by	lay-bys
	stand-by	stand-bys
	soliloquy	soliloquies
	money	*both* moneys *and* monies

Proper nouns generally retain **y**. *For example*

the Henrys, the Lackenbys, the Kennedys

4.5 There is no fixed system for the plural of nouns ending in **o**. Most familiar nouns ending in **o** add **es** to form the plural, but less familiar ones and others borrowed more recently from other languages add **s**.

For example

tomato	tomatoes
potato	potatoes
hero	heroes
go	goes
echo	echoes
dingo	dingoes
veto	vetoes
mosquito	mosquitoes
volcano	volcanoes
embargo	embargoes
motto	mottoes
photo	photos
avocado	avocados
solo	solos
yoyo	yoyos
manifesto	manifestos

fiasco	fiascos
kilo	kilos
proviso	provisos
quango	quangos
disco	discos
choko	chokos
ditto	dittos

As a word becomes more frequently used, its plural will mostly conform to the **es** plural. Consequently a considerable number of words, in the process of assimilation, are spelt with **s** or **es**. *For example*

memento, mango, grotto, innuendo, banjo, flamingo, lasso, salvo

Those having a vowel before the **o**, including those ending in **oo**, take only an **s**. *For example*

ratio	ratios
studio	studios
radio	radios
folio	folios
video	videos
embryo	embryos
zoo	zoos
boo	boos

Warning Do not use an apostrophe in the formation of plural nouns. More and more one sees the pernicious practice of an apostrophe used in the plural of words on signs. Beware especially with words ending in **o**: videos, photos, avocados, etc.

4.6 Special Cases

(a) A few common nouns have an irregular plural.

man	men	tooth	teeth
woman	women	foot	feet
ox	oxen	goose	geese
child	children	mouse	mice
brother	brethren *(in some cases)*	louse	lice

(b) A few words do not change for the plural. *For example*

sheep	fish
deer	trout
reindeer	salmon
grouse	bream *(and most other fish)*

▷

(c) Some nouns are plural in form and have no singular. *For example*

bellows	secateurs	billiards	measles
binoculars	shears	clothes	thanks
pants	spectacles	draughts	tidings
pliers	tongs	gallows	victuals
pyjamas	trousers	scissors	tweezers

Note

pyjama top	trouser leg
billiard cue	spectacle case
draught board	scissor blade

(d) Some nouns ending in **s** do not change in the plural. *For example*

species, innings, series

Words of French origin which end in a **silent s** have no change in the plural but the **s** is pronounced. *For example*

chassis, rendezvous, corps, fracas

(e) The following words have two plurals with different meanings.

brother	brothers *(same family)* brethren *(same society)*
craft	craft *(boats)* crafts *(handicrafts)*
genius	geniuses *(greatly talented)* genii *(spirits)*
index	indexes *(tables of contents)* indices *(algebraic exponents)*
medium	mediums *(at seances)* media *(newspapers, broadcasting, television)*

(f) *Observe* the plural of compound nouns of the following type.

daughters-in-law
men-of-war
aides-de-camp
governors-general
courts martial

(g) An apostrophe is used to form the plural of non-capitalised letters of the alphabet and single numbers. *For example*

i's, t's, s's, 4's, 6's

An apostrophe can be used with capital letters. *For example*

As or A's Xs or X's

It is not necessary to use an apostrophe with dates. *For example*

the 1920s, the 1980s

4.7 Words of foreign origin often retain their original plural. *Observe* the foreign patterns.

a becomes **ae** as in formulae, larvae, algae

a becomes **ata** as in stigmata, lemmata

is becomes **es** as in crises, axes, bases, neuroses, hypotheses

um becomes **a** as in errata, media, memoranda, strata, addenda

us becomes **i** as in stimuli, radii, alumni, fungi, cacti, gladioli

us becomes **era** as in genera

on becomes **a** as in phenomena, criteria

eau becomes **eaux** as in beaux, gateaux, bureaux, châteaux

eu becomes **eux** as in adieux, milieux

o becomes **i** as in virtuosi, maestri

ub and **ph** become **ubim** and **phim** as in cherubim, seraphim

ex and **ix** become **ices** as in indices, appendices, vortices, matrices

Some such words are however sometimes or more often used with an English plural. *For example*

formulas, memorandums, cherubs, syllabuses, ultimatums, indexes, cactuses, beaus, gateaus, virtuosos, adieus, bureaus

---

5 USE OF THE APOSTROPHE

5.1 To form the possessive of a noun, add **'s** (**apostrophe** *plus* **s**) to the noun. But when the noun ends in **s** then only an apostrophe is added; however, if in pronunciation an **s** sound is added to the sound of the original word, then **'s** must be added. *For example*

the boy's father	the boys' father
the woman's coat	the women's opponents
the lady's daughter	the ladies' umbrellas
the ass's head	the asses' path
Mr Ross's brother	the Rosses' party
Dickens's novels	the Joneses' car
the witness's testimony	the witnesses' testimony
the corps' insignia	the people's vote
the sheep's tracks	the two sheep's tracks
mathematics' discipline	the various species' habits
Richard III's successor	Edelbert the Younger's wife

Notice in the following that because an additional **s** is not sounded one is not written.

for convenience' sake
for appearance' sake
for goodness' sake

Notice also the avoidance of an awkward or clumsy pronunciation in an expression such as '*the three Mercedes' performance*'.

The names of stores today generally show no sign of ownership.

For example

at Woolworths
at Harrods
at Tiffanys

After the word **of**, the names of persons are almost always in the form with **'s**. *For example*

an idea of John's
an innings of Bradman's
that old car of Stephen's
a friend of Diana's

Notice also these expressions with pronouns.

a friend of mine
this land of ours

Observe the following.

the people opposite's garden
the woman upstairs' television

No comma is used in the following types of construction.

Tom Jones the singer's car
in front of Paul Stringer the butcher's house
on Lloyd Cameron the mayor's son's yacht

The apostrophe with **s** does not always of course indicate possession.

For example

the book's cover
the car's engine
today's problems
yesterday's festivities
our money's worth
at my wit's end
for heaven's sake

Notice some indefinite pronouns.

anyone's guess
no one's concern
someone else's idea

And

my wife's and my return
Anne and Lucy's mother
Anne's and Lucy's mother

An apostrophe is used with holidays and celebrations. *For example*

New Year's Day
Mother's Day
Father's Day
April Fools' Day

5.2 With the names of organisations and in other circumstances the apostrophe is not used, in modern practice, in such examples as the following where the sense of the noun is adjectival rather than possessive.

For example

Fort Street Boys High School
Senior Citizens Centre
United Nations Organisation
National Roads and Motorists Association
travellers cheques
the visitors book ▷

a government schools inspector
boys grade sport
ladies blouses
a mens fashion house
a seniors card

In most cases where the noun forms its plural irregularly the apostrophe is best retained, as also in the case of singular nouns. *For example*

Seamen's Mission
Children's Day
Women's Weekly
a driver's licence

For private institutions one should spell the name as it is spelt by the institution.

An apostrophe is generally not used with place names. *For example*

Kings Cross	Regents Park
St Marys	Thames Embankment

But an apostrophe is generally used with buildings. *For example*

Her Majesty's (*Theatre*), St Philip's (*Church*)

5.3 An apostrophe is used in phrases denoting a span of time or distance when the noun is singular, but increasingly the apostrophe is omitted with a plural noun. *For example*

a year's work
a month's notice
a fortnight's holiday
a night's rest
an hour's ride
a stone's throw

seven years hard labour
in four weeks time
a three months course
two minutes silence

5.4 *Note carefully*

I objected to Tom's going.
Prior to Tom's going ...
I objected to his going.

A point of grammar in reality, the possessive form is to be used in such expressions where the noun or pronoun stands between a preposition and the word form in *ing*. It is not a question of "I object to Tom" or "prior to Tom". When the expression is a complex one, the apostrophe is perhaps best omitted in order not to have the reader wondering what its purpose is.

5.5 A number of word contractions are normal in spoken English. The omission of the letter or letters is indicated by an apostrophe.

For example

it's	it is	don't	do not
I'm	I am	can't	cannot
there'll	there will	isn't	is not
they're	they are	won't	will not
we're	we are	didn't	did not
I've	I have	mustn't	must not
it'll	it will	doesn't	does not
we've	we have	shan't	shall not
he's	he is; he has	couldn't	could not
she's	she is; she has	shouldn't	should not
I'd	I would; I had	haven't	have not
we'd	we would; we had	hasn't	has not
I'll	I will; I shall	hadn't	had not
he'll	he will	you've	you have
she'll	she will	you're	you are
we'll	we will; we shall	'tis	it is
he'd	he would; he had	she'd	she would; she had

It is to be noted that these contractions should not be part of formal writing.

The use of contractions goes in speech beyond the combination of pronoun and verb, the verb and *not*, as shown above. *For example*

how'd	how would; how did
Betty's	Betty is; Betty has

Sometimes certain words suffer the loss of a letter in poetry for the sake of rhythm. The loss of the letter in question is indicated by an apostrophe. This practice should not be imitated in ordinary writing. However, in a very few fixed expressions it is normal for a letter to be suppressed and the suppression is likewise denoted by an apostrophe. *For example*

o'clock   ne'er-do-well   will-o'-the-wisp

An apostrophe is used to indicate the omission of the century in a date.

For example

the gay '90s
the roaring '20s
back in '69

5.6 Do not confuse the following:

its	*and*	it's (it is)
whose	*and*	who's (who is, who has)
your	*and*	you're (you are)
their	*and*	they're (they are) *or* there

The four words on the left *without the apostrophe* are the possessives!

Uses

Has the dog eaten its food?
No, it's still in the bowl.

Whose car is it?
Who's in the car?

Are they your running shoes?
So you're not taking them?

Where is their team?
I think they're over there.

The misuse of **it's** is without doubt the most common spelling error in the language. The possessive is spelt **its**.

The possessive pronouns **ours**, **yours**, **hers** and **theirs** have likewise no apostrophe.

6 CAPITAL LETTERS

6.1 A capital letter must be used at the beginning of a sentence.

6.2 A capital must be used for the first letter of names of people and personal titles. *For example*

Marlene Dietrich	the Prime Minister of Canada
Tom Cruise	the President of Italy
Mr Brown	the Governor of the Bahamas
Dr Bizewski	Lord Olivier
Dame Joan Sutherland	General Blamey
Her Majesty the Queen	Wilson D. Grantham III
the King of England	the Iron Lady
the Duke of Wellington	Ludwig van Beethoven

The initials of a person's name are not spaced. *For example*

J.B. Priestley
G.K. Chesterton

Notice that the latest military practice is not to hyphenate service titles.

For example

Lieutenant General Bourke
Flight Lieutenant Singh

But His Excellency the Governor-General

Notice that words of title like *president*, *governor*, *general*, *king*, when not used as a title do not have a capital letter. The same applies in plural references. *For example*

the kings of France
the prime ministers of Singapore
all the governors-general

6.3 A capital letter is used for nouns and adjectives of nationality.

For example

the British
the French
the Indonesian people
Russian *(language)*
the German chancellor
the Canadian border

6.4 A capital letter should be used for the names of countries and other places (towns, rivers, mountains, parks, streets). *For example*

France	San Francisco
Malta	Darling River
North America	Mount Everest
West Indies	Victoria Peak
South-East Asia	Collins Street
Northern Territory	Orchard Road
Edinburgh	Piccadilly Circus

But the Tigris and Euphrates rivers *(as combination)*

6.5 A capital should be used for the names of schools, colleges, organisations and buildings. *For example*

the University of London
Fort Street High School
the Federal Government
the Library of Congress
the Cabinet
Westminster Abbey
the Moulin Rouge
the Sydney Opera House
the Tate Gallery
Her Majesty's Theatre
the Savoy
the Taj Mahal

Observe that words such as *department*, *school*, *hotel*, when used on their own do not normally bear a capital.

6.6 Historical events, ceremonies and gatherings, government programmes, secular and religious holidays, are capitalised.

For example

the French Revolution
World War I
the Geneva Convention
the Olympic Games
the Edinburgh Festival
Ramadan
Anzac Day
Christmas Day
Hanukkah

6.7 A capital letter should be used in the titles of books, long poems, newspapers, magazines, films, musical works (operas, musical comedies, other music compositions with a descriptive title), paintings and sculptures, for the first word and all other words except the articles (*the*, *a*, *an*), prepositions (*by*, *in*, *at*, *with*, *of*, *through*, etc.) and conjunctions (*and*, *if*, *as*, *but*, etc.). The title should be underlined in writing and italicised in print. *For example*

Alice in Wonderland
Treasure Island
Pilgrim's Progress
War and Peace
Paradise Lost
The *Straits Times*
The *Sydney Morning Herald*
Paris Match
The *New Yorker*
Gone with the Wind
Doctor Zhivago
Rain Man
Star Wars
It Happened One Night
The Phantom of the Opera
The Merry Widow
The Mastersingers of Nuremberg
Blue Poles
The Night Watch
Mona Lisa
The Thinker

Note

(a) A definite article forming the first word of the title of a newspaper is not underlined or italicised. A definite or indefinite article forming the first word of any title is omitted if the reading would be awkward with its inclusion,

(b) The word *Bible*, the names of the books of the Bible and other sacred books are always spelt with a capital or capitals. Neither italics nor inverted commas are used. *For example*

Acts of the Apostles
Book of Isaiah
New Testament
Koran

(c) The chapters or sections of books, magazines etc., lectures, songs, short poems, radio and television programmes, are capitalised as for other titles and placed in double inverted commas.

6.8 A capital letter or letters should be used for the names of ships, cars, trains, aeroplanes and spacecraft. Italics are used for specific items, but not for brand names. *For example*

Titanic	Concorde
HMAS *Melbourne*	Boeing 767
QE2	BMW
Bluebird	Mazda 323
Flying Scotsman	Rolls-Royce
Southern Cross	Chevrolet
Atlantis	Harley-Davidson
Voyager II	Kawasaki

6.9 The days of the week and the months of the year bear a capital.

The formal rendition of a date is: 1 April 1850; 31 December 1997.

A capital should not be used for the seasons or compass points (unless included in a name). *For example*

in spring	to the north
after winter	from the south-west

6.10 A capital is also used:

To begin direct speech;

To begin each line of poetry (as traditional practice);

In forms of address such as Dad, Mum, Doctor;

For the pronouns *He*, *Him*, *His*, *Who*, etc. when the pronoun refers to God or Christ, although some modern practice dispenses with a capital;

For the word *I*;

At the beginning of a letter after *Dear*: Dear Sir, Dear Madam;

To personify an abstract quality, a device most often occurring in poetry.

Note Computer language and advertising have brought unusual forms of spelling with a capital letter in the middle of a word such as *WordStar*, *WorkCare*, *CinemaScope*, *PolyGram*.

Trade names should be spelt with a capital letter but most often are not.

Apart from obligatory uses of capitals, there are cases where a capital letter might well be used for effect in order to draw attention to a word or set of words. The advice is however given not to use capitals all over the place. Always have a valid reason – be sparing of their non-obligatory use.

Some few words need at times to have a capital in the cause of clarity or for some specific reason. Amongst the most common of these are: state/State, earth/Earth, church/Church, power/Power, act/Act. *For example*

> Pollution is damaging the earth in this area.
> Pollution is endangering our Earth.

Block capitals are used frequently throughout the text in advertising. It is to be noted that an apostrophe is often suppressed in such usage.

Special Note Scientific nomenclature needs special attention.

For example when animals and plants are referred to with their Latin names, the genus stands in italics with capital letter and the species (and subspecies) in uncapitalised italics.

Hippopotamus amphibius	hippopotamus
Antirrhinum majus	snapdragon
Apium graveolens	celery
Eucalyptus pauciflora	snowgum

These examples are but four of a vast range of scientific expressions. There are countless others in the technical and computer fields, examination of which lies beyond this basic presentation.

7 USE OF THE HYPHEN

There is no general fixed rule for the use of the hyphen between words. One cannot just pick up any dictionary and find the final solution there. In many cases, the combination you want to use will not be found in any dictionary. The study of different dictionaries will show that the use is far from being clearly established. Some dictionaries have a liking for the hyphen, others not.

Beyond this, there is great variation in the use of the hyphen in English. One has to steer one's way between the dictionaries. The reader is well advised to consult them. Dictionaries will, however, even seem to take delight in contradicting themselves. The one dictionary, by way of example, presents the spellings: *lunch hour*, *lunch-break*, *lunchtime*; *tea caddy*, *tea-tray*, *teacup*; *news stall*, *news-sheet*, *newsstand*. Perhaps with good reason? And here is the crux of the dilemma. Do I spell the idea as two separate words? Do I link the words together with a hyphen? Or do I join them together as one word? For such is the problem in quite a number of cases. It is to be hoped that what follows will be of some assistance in dealing with this rather tricky aspect of English spelling.

Some cases of the hyphen are quite clear: *a high chair*, *a high-chair*; *twenty odd actors*, *twenty-odd actors*; *more experienced staff*, *more-experienced staff*; *in flight movies*, *in-flight movies*. In these very clear examples can be seen the basis of the solution. A hyphen is not a decorative device. Like other punctuation marks, it is to be used to assist the reader by making the reading as clear as possible.

If the reading is clear without a hyphen, the best advice is that none should be used. If however the first word needs to be tied to the following in the cause of clarity (because the two words constitute an idea and there is a possibility of separation for whatever reason), a hyphen is used. Some combinations, especially of one-syllable words, may in time through frequent use become a single word. Much depends on what happens in the appearance of the *combined* word. If the meaning cannot be readily seen because consonants and vowels are *mixed up* in the middle of the word, a hyphen is best used. Again the best advice is to reduce the use of a hyphen to the minimum, but use one when a hyphen is necessary for clarity.

A few concrete words of advice can be given with regard to certain situations.

But remember the important point that the situation is ever changing as combinations of words are more frequently used with time.

7.1 Nouns of the following type, made up of an adverb and a verb, are one word. *For example*

input, bypass, downpour, onset, upsurge

But in the case of nouns made up of a verb and adverb, the compound is usually found with a hyphen except when there is no clash of vowel or distracting effect. *For example*

send-off	lay-by	stopover
make-up	sell-out	breakthrough
drive-in	shoot-out	runaway
hold-up	take-off	playoff

The corresponding verbs are always written as two words. *For example*

to take off	to pass by
to make up	to drive in

Observe most carefully the following.

The setting-up of a commission was called for.
His setting up a commission quickly followed.
Shortly after its setting-up, the commission experienced problems.

7.2 Most compound nouns that are made up of at least one noun will be written as one word or two words. Only when the two elements are of equal status or when the compound is a triplet will a hyphen be used.

For example

airline	red tape
sweatshirt	black market
runway	post office
locksmith	coffee table
viewpoint	sales talk
playboy	bargain store
bedroom	swan song
teacup	punctuation mark
schoolchild	exercise book
lampshade	cricket team
wheelbarrow	government aid
blackmail	adult education
outpatient	television station
roadblock	generation gap
pickpocket	washing machine
globetrotter	flying saucer
weedkiller	frying pan
shoplifting	writing pad
sightseeing	playing field
stocktaking	living wage

▷

owner-driver	give-and-take
walkie-talkie	daughter-in-law
hurdy-gurdy	hand-me-down

But a considerable number of words are nonetheless normally written with a hyphen. *For example*

engine-room	cross-section
tea-break	name-dropper
eye-level	by-election
she-oak	press-box
heart-throb	post-mortem
off-chance	centre-forward
wicket-keeper	machine-gun

In fact, a great number of compound nouns of differing patterns are used with a hyphen. *For example*

know-how	get-together	has-been
shut-eye	hot-shot	look-see

Note To avoid ambiguity, a hyphen is needed at times.

stock exchange report
shire council rates
adult education fees
higher adult-education fees
higher education fees
higher-education fees

7.3 Most compound adverbs are written as one word. *For example*

upstream	overboard	bareback

7.4 The following types of compound adjectives are almost always hyphenated.

red-hot	hot-headed
icy-cold	short-winded
large-scale	heavy-handed
trouble-free	fair-haired

forty-hour	second-class
eleventh-hour	third-rate
75-year-old	first-named
20th-century	last-mentioned

a reddish-brown coat
a canary-yellow dress
black-and-white photography

Compare black-and-white tiles
black and white tiles

Note Some expressions will be found with three hyphens. *For example*

up-to-the-minute information
a once-in-a-lifetime opportunity
state-of-the-art technology

7.5 When in a compound adjective the second element is a present participle or a past participle, the compound almost always bears a hyphen. *For example*

good-looking	muscle-bound
ear-shattering	panic-stricken
pleasure-seeking	rough-hewn
hard-working	short-lived
heart-rending	half-baked
record-breaking	guilt-ridden
awe-inspiring	hand-woven
well-meaning	far-fetched
fact-finding	hard-won
award-winning	battle-scarred

Note gold medal-winning team

But notice such words as the following.

ongoing	spellbinding	widespread
forthcoming	crestfallen	airborne

When an adjective compound consists, however, of the adverb *well*, *ill*, *much* or *little* and a past participle, a hyphen is used when the compound comes in front of the noun but generally not when it is used predicatively (after the noun or pronoun). *For example*

She is a well-known actor.
As an actor she is well known.

It is an ill-conceived plan.
The plan was ill conceived.

Enrico was a much-loved man.
His daughters were also much loved.

They set off along a little-used path.
The cabin appeared little used. ▷

Observe that a hyphen is not used if the participle is preceded by a comparative or superlative form or if the adverb itself is modified.

For example

the most acclaimed novel
better known players
the worst devastated areas
the more advanced nations
the least afflicted villages
a very well maintained house

7.6 Some adjective compounds consist of short phrases. These are hyphenated when standing in front of the noun but usually not if used predicatively (after the noun), although practice varies according to the nature of the expression. *For example*

up-to-date	on-site	cast-off
well-to-do	hand-to-mouth	made-up
out-of-pocket	spot-on	thrown-out

I want an up-to-date report.
Is your homework up to date?

There is a great variety of such adjective compounds, some of which can be used only in front of a noun. *For example*

a tax-deductible contribution
a trade-in valuation
a wake-up call
a devil-may-care attitude
an all-too-frequent occurrence

Note When in a title or heading a capital is to be used for the first member of a hyphenated word, whether the second is to be capitalised depends upon its importance in relation to the first.

For example

Space-Age Technology
Last-minute Proposals
Peace-making Mission

7.7 Prefixes almost always followed by a hyphen:

When **all**, **ever**, **ex**, **half**, **non**, **quasi**, **self** or **vice** are used as prefixes, a hyphen follows. *For example*

all-electric	non-event
all-important	non-proliferation
all-rounder	non-returnable
ever-helpful	non-smoking

ever-present
ex-convict
ex-serviceman
ex-wife
half-back
half-forgotten
half-hour
half-hourly
half-sister
non-viable
quasi-academic
quasi-official
self-criticism
self-discipline
self-made
self-service
vice-president
vice-admiral

Except everlasting
half pay, half holiday; halfpenny
nonsense, nonplus, nondescript, nonentity, nonconformist
selfless, selfsame
viceroy, viceregal

7.8 Prefixes mostly attached:

The prefixes **co**, **counter**, **extra**, **out**, **over**, **sub**, **under**, are mostly joined on, but in a few words they are mostly found with a hyphen.
For example

coexist	co-author
coefficient	co-producer
counteract	counter-productive
counterpart	counter-revolutionary
extraordinary	extra-sensory
extramural	extra-marital
outdo	out-swinger
outdated	out-tray
oversight	over-sensitive
overdue	over-confidence
subdivision	sub-branch
subconscious	sub-editor
underwater	under-estimate
undercurrent	under-age

The jumbles that appear in some dictionaries are better written with a hyphen. And it is stressed that it is in this area that dictionaries are most at variance with one another.

7.9 A hyphen is also used to avoid the juxtaposition of two **e**'s (in such words as *re-examine*, *re-entry*) or two **o**'s (in such words as *co-opt*, *co-operate*). *For example*

re-edit	pre-eminent	co-ordinate
re-establish	pre-emptory	co-ordinator

But skiing, taxiing

Further, prefixes (mostly ending in a vowel) that are not normally followed by a hyphen take one when the word to which they are attached begins with a vowel. *For example*

pre-arrange	semi-invalid
anti-aircraft	semi-automatic
auto-immune	post-operative

But predate, predisposed
antisocial, anticlockwise
autobiography, autopilot
semifinal, semicircular
postdate, postscript, postgraduate

Different vowels are otherwise juxtaposed. *For example*

coequal, reaffirm, reorganise, reunification, coincidence, coeducation, radioactive, psychoanalyse

---

7.10 Special Cases

(a) Prefixes that are not normally followed by a hyphen take one when the word to which they are joined begins with a capital letter.

For example

un-American	anti-Japanese
pro-British	pre-Second World War

Note also:

T-shirt	pre-1960
H-bomb	post-1980
V-neck	
X-ray	

(b) A hyphen is also used to distinguish *re-cover* from *recover*, *re-count* from *recount*, etc. *For example*

re-lay, relay	re-treat, retreat
re-sign, resign	re-bound, rebound
re-form, reform	re-strain, restrain
re-sort, resort	re-creation, recreation

7.11 Numbers from 21 to 99 (except the tens) and fractions are hyphenated. *For example*

eighty-nine	one-quarter
sixty-six	two-tenths

7.12 Breaking a Word

Sometimes only part of a full word is written as in cases such as *four- or fivefold, long- and short-term interest*. In such cases a hyphen must be used.

When a word is broken at the end of a line, a hyphen must be used at the end of the top line. It is strongly advised never to split words because the practice can baulk the meaning; but if there must be a break, the word should be broken logically so that the reader is not misled. In fact the reader should be able to guess what is on the next line.

Bear in mind that it may be necessary to divide long words at different points. In the guidelines below, only the preferred division is shown in each section.

Guidelines Do not divide words of fewer than six letters;
Have at least three letters on each line;
A divided word should not end a page (right or left).

Break a hyphenated word at the hyphen, and a non-hyphenated compound at the point of union

Divide off an affix (prefix or suffix): dis-appear, honour-able.

Break between double consonants: accom-modation, insuf-ferable.

Break between two or more consonants according to pronunciation: pic-ture, prob-lem, cele-brate, volu-ble, pre-scribe.

A single consonant is usually taken over, but preserve the base of a word: thou-sand, popu-lar, gri-mace; pun-ish, col-our.

With forms in *-ing*, only the *ing* will be taken over in most words: miss-ing, tir-ing, hurry-ing; chuck-ling, puz-zling.

Do not divide two consonants that form one sound: calm-est, laugh-able; never divide *ch* or *ck*: mer-chant, pack-aged.

Watch that a false pronunciation does not result: criti-cism, espe-cially.

Divide between two vowels only when they are sounded separately: humili-ate.

Do not break before a vowel that itself forms a syllable: uni-versal, vio-late.

8 SHORTENED FORMS

8.1 The principle for approved contractions is that no full stop is used when the final letter of the shortened word is used as the last letter of the shortened form. *For example*

Mr Stark	Messrs Macarthur
Mrs Stark	Grace Bros *(Brothers)*
Dr Cattaruzzi	Hollywood Blvd
St Joseph	Gipps St
Sr Marie Bernarde	Cardinal Ave
Maths	Rm 303 (*Room 303*)

As a shortened form, a contraction is to be distinguished from an abbreviation. The final letter of an abbreviation is a letter other than the last letter of the word.

8.2 If the final letter of the shortened form is not used as the last letter of the abbreviation, a full stop is used. *For example*

Capt. Bligh	Captain Bligh
Gen. Grant	General Grant
Prof. Robinson	Professor Robinson
R.J. Pappas Esq.	R.J. Pappas Esquire
M. Poirot	Monsieur Poirot
Mon.	Monday
Aug.	August

The abbreviation of a person's first name however bears no full stop. *For example*

Kev *(Kevin)* Allen
Dot *(Dorothy)* Montrone
Rob *(Robert)* Lowe

8.3 There are hundreds and hundreds of shortened forms made up of the first letters of words written with capitals. *For example*

M.P.	Member of Parliament
P.M.	Prime Minister
M.L.A.	Member of Legislative Assembly
B.A.	Bachelor of Arts
M.B.A.	Master of Business Administration
U.S.A.	United States of America
B.B.C.	British Broadcasting Corporation
N.Z.	New Zealand
N.S.W.	New South Wales
R.A.A.F.	Royal Australian Air Force
E.U.	European Union
U.N.	United Nations

G.P.O.	General Post Office
M.M.	Military Medal
Y.M.C.A.	Young Men's Christian Association
I.S.B.N.	International Standard Book Number
U.N.E.S.C.O.	United Nations Educational, Scientific, and Cultural Organisation
N.A.S.A.	National Aeronautics and Space Administration
A.I.D.S.	Acquired Immune Deficiency Syndrome

Note The M.P.'s secretary

Abbreviations of the above type, which consist of only capital letters, are often today written without full stops. *For example*

BA	USA	RAAF	ISBN
MM	MLA	BBC	UNESCO

Observe also the mixed type. *For example*

Dip.Ed.	DipEd	Diploma in Education
Ph.D.	PhD	Doctor of Philosophy

Be careful not to insert an apostrophe into the plural of an abbreviation.

M.M.s or MMs	Military Medals
M.P.s or MPs	Members of Parliament

Note the M.P.s' special allowance

An acronym (a shortened form, usually made up of initials, that is always pronounced as a word) as it becomes more well known may be used with only an initial capital. *For example*

Anzac, Qantas, Unesco, Nasa

Notice the mixed practice with shortened forms of the States of Australia.

Vic.	(VIC)	Victoria
Tas.	(TAS)	Tasmania
Qld	(QLD)	Queensland
N.S.W.	(NSW)	New South Wales
S.A.	(SA)	South Australia
W.A.	(WA)	Western Australia
N.T.	(NT)	Northern Territory

Notice also that *Q.* is now much used for Queensland and that the regionalised form *F.N.Q.* for Far North Queensland is current. The form *V.* for Victoria is also coming into use.

The form *Cwlth* is used for Commonwealth.

8.4 Other abbreviations are formed from the first letters of words written with small letters. *For example*

a.m.	before noon (Latin *ante meridiem)*
p.m.	after noon (Latin *post meridiem)*
a.s.a.p.	as soon as possible
n.a.	not applicable
o.s.	overseas
t.b.a.	to be advised
a.k.a.	also known as

Sometimes capitals occur in the abbreviation when words do not ordinarily have a capital. At times the abbreviation is formed of letters taken from a phrase or parts of a word, although the origin may lie in a technical term or in a foreign language.

U.F.O.	unidentified flying object
P.O.W.	prisoner of war
C.O.D.	cash on delivery
J.I.T.	just in time
MS.	manuscript
T.B.	tuberculosis
S.S.W.	south-south-west
R.S.V.P.	please answer (French *répondez s'il vous plaît)*
O.K.	okay
I.O.U.	I owe you
SOS	save our souls
P.T.O.	please turn over *(page)*
T.V.	television
V.C.R.	video cassette recorder
C.D.	compact disc
H.P.	hire purchase
XL	extra large *(clothing size)*
A4	A series, size 4 *(paper size – 297 x 210 mm)*
M.S.G.	monosodium glutamate
BBQ	barbecue

8.5 Literary terms frequently have abbreviated forms. From Latin in particular many abbreviations have been formed. *For example*

vol.	volume
fig.	figure
adj.	adjective
pl.	plural
l.	line
p.	page
f.	folio; following page, verse, etc.

v. *or* vs	versus, against
ibid.	in the same work *(ibidem)*
etc.	and so on *(et cetera)*
cf.	compare *(confer)*
i.e.	that is *(id est)*
e.g.	for example *(exempli gratia)*
q.v.	which see *(quod vide)*
N.B.	take careful note *(nota bene)*
P.S.	postscript *(postscriptum)*

Observe also the representation of the word *number* by *no*. (Italian *numero*). A full stop is used to differentiate it from the word *no*. A capital letter is required only if it stands with an expression in capitals. A space is used before the following number(s): no. 7, pp. 31-5

8.6 The plural of a literary abbreviation is normally formed with **s**, the full stop falling away as **s** would be the last letter of the word contracted. *For example*

vols nos figs

The plural of abbreviations consisting of one letter is formed by repeating the letter of the singular form. *For example*

ll. pp. ff.

8.7 *Notice* that there are other fields where similar abbreviated forms are used. *For example*

log.	logarithm	p.a.	per annum *(for each year)*
sq.	square	h.p.	horsepower
pop.	population	r.p.m.	revolutions per minute

But notice trigonometrical functions: sin *(sine)*, cos *(cosine)*

Note The identical abbreviated form may stand for different expressions, with appropriate meaning in the particular field. *For example*

v.	versus *(against)*
v.	velocity
v.	verse
v.	verb
v.	vide (Latin *see)*

Note also P.A. Press Association; public address system; personal assistant

N.A.S. National Association of Schoolmasters; Noise Abatement Society

▷

Classified ads in newspapers and magazines are a particular example of shortened forms. Each area has its own peculiar usage for going about saving space and money. Out of their specific contexts such abbreviations are devoid of meaning. *For example*

> Recently renov. 1 b.r. unfurn. unit, parq. flr, o/s. pkg, lndry facs, fresh paint. Handy to all amens.

8.8 Chemical Symbols

The symbols of chemical elements do not have a full stop. They are not abbreviations but internationally recognised representations. *For example*

H	hydrogen	K	potassium *(kalium)*
O	oxygen	Mn	manganese
H_2O	water	Au	gold *(aurum)*

8.9 Metric Measurement Symbols

The symbols of metric measurements are likewise written without a full stop and no ***s*** is used in the plural. The symbol is today usually written against the number. *For example*

15mm	fifteen millimetres
1cm	one centimetre
5cm	five centimetres
45m	forty-five metres
8km	eight kilometres
500g	500 grams
100kg	one hundred kilograms
3t	three tonnes
10L	ten litres
300mL	three hundred millilitres
$4m^2$	four square metres
30cc	thirty cubic centimetres
80gsm	eighty grams per square metre
25c	twenty-five cents
7kW	seven kilowatts

Non-metric measurements also generally today take no sign of the plural, and in conformity with metric measurements all are doubtless best written without a full stop. *For example*

2in	two inches
14ft	fourteen feet
200yd	two hundred yards
loz	one ounce
1½lb	one and a half pounds

3cwt	three hundredweight
6pt	six pints
2qt	two quarts
15gal	fifteen gallons
30fm	thirty fathoms

8.10 Currency Codes

Many countries have their own symbol for their currency, e.g. £ denotes Pound Sterling (Great Britain) and ¥ denotes Yen (Japan). Some countries use the same term for their currency and use similar symbols. For example, the Dollar in the United States is $ (note the two vertical strokes through the capital S), while in Australia we recognise $ (note the single vertical stroke through the capital S).

Currency traders, who rely on computer generated text, are however limited to the alphabet when denoting a currency. As a consequence, with the use of capital letters, certain combinations of letters have been formalised into SWIFT codes (Society for Worldwide Interbank Financial Telecommunication). This is the code system used in international currency exchange.

While it is correct to denote one thousand Australian dollars as $1000.00, it is usually written as AUD 1000.00. The following list is exemplary of the most commonly used SWIFT codes.

AUD	Australian Dollar	SEK	Swedish Kroner
USD	United States Dollar	SGD	Singapore Dollar
JPY	Japanese Yen	NLG	Dutch Guilder
DEM	German Deutschmark	NOK	Norwegian Kroner
GBP	British Pound	HKD	Hong Kong Dollar
CHF	Swiss Franc	ITL	Italian Lire
FRS	French Franc	BEF	Belgian Franc *(financial)*
CAD	Canadian Dollar	PTS	Spanish Peseta
NZD	New Zealand Dollar	GRD	Greek Drachma

8.11 Other Symbols

©	copyright	@	at
®	registered	&	and *(ampersand)*
™	trade mark	#	number *or* space

There are also symbols used as correction marks in proofing text.

For example

^	insert	CAPS	capital letters
stet	leave as is	ital	italic

9 SPELLING WATCHPOINTS

9.1 Words with the Same Pronunciation

Many words in English with the same pronunciation are spelt differently. Those listed below are merely some examples.

here	hear	red	read
great	grate	fourth	forth
led	lead	see	sea
waste	waist	horse	hoarse
board	bored	fair	fare
loan	lone	pain	pane
bear	bare	gate	gait
pale	pail	die	dye
break	brake	night	knight
groan	grown	story	storey
bark	barque	bow	bough
birth	berth	threw	through
hoard	horde	past	passed
tire	tyre	flower	flour
tail	tale	done	dun
choir	quire	throws	throes
plane	plain	might	mite
stayed	staid	slight	sleight
dear	deer	ring	wring
feet	feat	read	reed
air	heir	peel	peal
wait	weight	course	coarse
caught	court	rest	wrest
beach	beech	fur	fir
real	reel	heard	herd
wave	waive	faint	feint
stair	stare	meat	meet
sail	sale	missed	mist
seen	scene	male	mail
ate	eight	blue	blew
to	two, too	sew	so, sow
buy	by, bye	rain	rein, reign
for	four, fore	prays	praise, preys
road	rode, rowed	wrapped	rapped, rapt
right	write, rite	pair	pear, pare

9.2 Words with the Same Spelling

Many different words in English have the same spelling. Almost all have the same pronunciation.

For example			*Exceptions*
mine	jar	hide	lead
grave	dear	stole	bow
start	bark	fence	row
light	peer	ring	tear
saw	loaf	duck	sow
pine	fleet	bank	refuse
coach	left	mean	close
league	pelt	page	minute
bear	kind	rear	entrance
rare	fine	lean	desert

For useful reference, make a list of other words of these types that you come across.

9.3 Words with Two Accepted Spellings

A few words have two generally accepted spellings. One of these might well run counter to the rules outlined herein. Neither can be said in most cases to be preferred. For you the advice is *just follow the rules*.

For example

judgement	judgment
lodgement	lodgment
acknowledgement	acknowledgment
ageing	aging
moveable	movable
likeable	likable
liveable	livable
sizeable	sizable
deductable	deductible
collectable	collectible
enquiry	inquiry
despatch	dispatch
extrovert	extravert
align	aline
flyer	flier
biased	biassed
focusing	focussing

9.4 American Spelling

(a) There is no preference, with regard to correctness, for the **ise** or **ize** ending in the appropriate words. It is just that the **ise** form is more common in British writing and the Americans prefer the **ize** spelling. *For example*

organise	organize
organisation	organization

Remember however that some words have to be spelt with **ise** and a few with **ize**. *(See Section 1.2)*

(b) In American spelling the letter **l** does not double as indicated for English spelling when endings are added, so the following words (as examples) would appear in American books with only one **l**: traveller, dialling, counsellor, woollen, marvellous.

But some words are to be found in American English with a **double l** where only one **l** is found in British usage: enrolment, instalment, skilful, wilful, etc.

(c) The reader should be careful not to imitate correct American practice. There is a considerable number of other differences, particularly the American predilection for dropping the **u** in **our** words. Americans also use **er** rather than **re** at the end of words such as *centre*, *theatre*. Further words with a different American spelling are *defence*, *cheque*, *tyre*, *programme*, presented only as a few of many.

It is also pointed out that Americans use many words differently. The American pronunciation of some words is also different.

Further, certain words are quite commonly used in American parlance and writing that are virtually unknown outside of America.

Advice is given to follow at all times the rules laid down in *Spelling English* in order not to end up with a hotchpotch of British and American forms.

9.5 Silent Letters

The English language is rather rich in words in which a silent letter lurks – or even a couple. There can be no rule for silent letters, but the reader's attention must be drawn to their existence. The words listed below are merely some examples.

pharaoh	through	mnemonic
bomb	thorough	autumn
thumb	insight	condemn
subtle	honour	hymn

doubt	ghost	touch
czar	jodhpurs	tough
indict	gingham	psychology
yacht	exhaust	pneumonia
Wednesday	straight	island
adjudicate	parliament	mortgage
pleurisy	knob	listen
rheumatism	knife	trait
gnarled	blackguard	gauge
reign	embalm	fourth
malign	salmon	wreck

9.6 Accents – Spelling Marks

Various languages employ *accent* marks in the spelling to indicate vowel quality, thus distinguishing one sound from another. These marks normally have nothing to do with the stress on a syllable. Sometimes they serve to distinguish the meaning of two otherwise identically spelt words. In other usages, the accent sign may merely denote the loss of a letter.

The English language has borrowed many words from different languages and so a few notes on the behaviour of borrowed words with accents will be found useful. In this regard the French language is the most important because of the number of borrowed French words and because of the frequent occurrence of accents in French words.

In many instances although the use of a certain French word may be accepted in English, the word is not yet regarded as an English word. In these cases the French accent sign is used in the English spelling and the word is often found printed in *italics* in English dictionaries – *rosé*, *crème*, *curé*, etc. Other French words are regarded as fully part of the English vocabulary. In such cases the spelling is by no means fixed. While some may have lost their accent *(gateau, regisseur,* etc.), others usually retain the accent in the spelling *(château, crêpe, résumé,* etc.). In some cases the spelling both with and without the French accent is acceptable *(rôle, role; regime, régime;* etc.).

With regard to the actual accents used, French has three basic accent marks. These three are placed above the appropriate vowel.

acute (ˊ)	indicating a close **e** sound *(résumé)*
grave (ˋ)	indicating an open **e** sound (*crème*)
circumflex (ˆ)	indicating in the case of some vowels a differing pronunciation *(vôtre, votre)* ▷

Other Accent Marks

cedilla (̧)	placed under a **c**, indicating that the **c** has the sound of **s** *(façade)*
umlaut (¨)	two dots over a vowel in German, indicating a different vowel sound from that of the letter without them *(Röntgen)*
tilde (˜)	placed over a letter, as over the letter **n** in Spanish, indicating a palatal nasal sound *(señor)* like *ny*
diaeresis (¨)	two dots placed over a vowel, indicating that it is separately sounded *(naïve)*

In languages other than French the acute accent has different functions. In English the grave sign indicates distinct syllabic value although it is not part of the spelling *(belovèd)*. It is also to be noted that earlier some of these accent signs had other functions in certain languages. Other accents are also in use today.

Two signs to be found above vowels in dictionaries denote the length of the vowel. They have nothing to do with the word's spelling.

macron (¯)	a short horizontal line, indicating that the vowel is a long sound
breve (˘)	a hook, indicating that the vowel is a short sound

Note also that the use of the acute sign, placed *after* a letter in a dictionary, is merely to indicate syllabic stress. It is *not* part of the spelling.

9.7 Letter Writing

The correct procedure for the beginning of a formal letter is as follows.

Note the comma.

Dear Sir,
Dear Madam,

The text of the letter begins on the next line one letter space in from the comma.

Practice varies for the beginning of any following paragraph. The paragraph is most often inset as far as the first paragraph. Or then again it may be begun on the margin or set in five letter spaces. In some practice, especially in the case of typed letters, all paragraphs are begun on the left margin.

The ending of a formal letter is with the words:

Yours faithfully,
Signature

Notice the word *faithfully* has a small letter, not a capital.

The same practice applies in the case of a personal letter with such terms as those below.

Yours sincerely,

or

Yours truly,

or

Kind regards,

Personal letters may of course end with more endearing terms.

9.8 The problem of **a** v. **an**

(a) The form **a** is used before all consonants except silent **h**.

For example

a man
a woman
a hysterical woman
a history

But an hour
an honourable man

(b) The form **an** is used before vowels. *For example*

an umbrella
an orange
an ache
an only son
an onerous burden

However the form **a** is used before a vowel if there is the sounding of **y** or **w**. *For example*

a unit *(y* sound*)*
a unique style *(y* sound*)*
a eulogy *(y* sound*)*
a one-time mayor *(w* sound*)*
such a one as he *(w* sound*)*

Note The form **an** is still sometimes used before words beginning with sounded **h** in an unstressed syllable. *For example*

an hypothesis
an historical treatise

9.9 Morse Code

The Morse code is a telegraphic alphabet used for signalling messages when no spoken or written communication is possible. The letters of the alphabet are represented by combinations of dots and dashes for transmission as short and long electrical contacts, sounds, flashes, etc. The system is named after its inventor Samuel Morse.

A	.–	**N**	–.	**1**	.––––
B	–...	**O**	–––	**2**	..–––
C	–.–.	**P**	.––.	**3**	...––
D	–..	**Q**	––.–	**4**	....–
E	.	**R**	.–.	**5**	.....
F	..–.	**S**	...	**6**	–....
G	––.	**T**	–	**7**	––...
H	....	**U**	..–	**8**	–––..
I	..	**V**	...–	**9**	––––.
J	.–––	**W**	.––	**0**	–––––
K	–.–	**X**	–..–		
L	.–..	**Y**	–.––		
M	––	**Z**	––..		

9.10 Phonetic Alphabet Code

Because the names of the letters of the alphabet can be easily confused when they are spoken, a system of clue words to represent the letters is in use to ensure no misunderstanding. The commonest experiences for most people are in watching television word games or when reciting the licence plate number of a motor vehicle such as NXD 250 *(November, X-ray, Delta 250)* according to the table below.

A	ALPHA	**J**	JULIET	**S**	SIERRA
B	BRAVO	**K**	KILO	**T**	TANGO
C	CHARLIE	**L**	LIMA	**U**	UNIFORM
D	DELTA	**M**	MIKE	**V**	VICTOR
E	ECHO	**N**	NOVEMBER	**W**	WHISKEY
F	FOXTROT	**O**	OSCAR	**X**	X-RAY
G	GOLF	**P**	PAPA	**Y**	YANKEE
H	HOTEL	**Q**	QUEBEC	**Z**	ZULU
I	INDIA	**R**	ROMEO		

This system is regularly used in military settings for the communication of grid references. The phonetic alphabet is also in use within the aviation industry worldwide. Previously other words have been used.

9.11 Can You Differentiate?

As a test of your spelling ability and your knowledge of English, can you differentiate between the meaning or the use of the following pairs or sets of words?

accede, exceed
accept, except
access, excess
accessory, accessary
adapt, adopt
adapter, adaptor, adopter
addition, edition
adverse, averse
advice, advise
affect, effect
affection, affectation
afflict, inflict
aid, aide
air, heir
airy, eerie, eyrie
aisle, isle
allay, alley, ally
allude, elude
allusion, illusion, delusion
aloud, allowed
alter, altar
alternative, alternate
angel, angle
annex, annexe
antique, antic
appreciative, appreciable
arc, ark
armour, amour
ascent, assent
ascetic, acetic, aesthetic
augur, auger
bail, bale
baited, bated
ball, bawl
ballet, ballot
balmy, barmy
bark, barque
barren, baron
base, bass
bath, bathe
bazaar, bizarre
beach, beech
bear, bare
beer, bier
bell, belle
benevolent, beneficial, beneficent
biannual, biennial
birth, berth
block, bloc
blond, blonde
blue, blew
board, bored
border, boarder
bore, boar, boor
born, borne
bow, bough
boy, buoy
break, brake
breeches, breaches
bridal, bridle
brim, bream
broach, brooch
bury, berry
but, butt, butte
buy, by, bye
calendar, colander
cannon, canon
can't, cant
canter, cantor
canvas, canvass
carrot, carat, caret
cart, carte
carton, cartoon
cast, caste
ceiling, sealing
censor, censure, censer, sensor ▷

cent, sent, scent
chased, chaste
check, cheque
choir, quire
civility, servility
climatic, climactic
climb, clime
cloth, clothe
college, collage
colonel, kernel
comma, coma
compare, compere, compeer
compliment, complement
confident, confidant
consistency, constancy
construct, construe
contagious, contiguous
contemptible, contemptuous
continuous, continual
coral, choral
cord, chord
corpse, corps, copse
council, counsel
counsellor, councillor
course, coarse
court, caught
courtesy, curtsy
credible, creditable, credulous
creek, creak
crevice, crevasse
critic, critique
curb, kerb
currant, current
cygnet, signet
dairy, diary
dear, deer
decent, descent, dissent
defect, deflect
deficient, defective
demur, demure
dependent, dependant
depository, depositary
depreciate, deprecate
desert, dessert
detract, distract
device, devise
die, dye
difference, deference
discomfort, discomfit
discreet, discrete
discuss, discus
disease, decease
distinct, distinctive
diverse, divers
done, dun
dose, doze
draft, draught
dragon, dragoon
dual, duel
dying, dyeing
economic, economical
educationist, educationalist
effectual, efficacious
efficient, effective
elicit, illicit
eligible, illegible
emigrant, immigrant
eminent, imminent, immanent
emolument, emollient
enumerate, enunciate
envelop, envelope
equable, equitable
errand, errant, arrant
erratic, erotic
exercise, exorcise
existent, existential
expandable, expendable
expatriate, expatiate
expedient, expeditious
extent, extant
exterminate, extenuate
facetious, factious, fictitious
faint, feint
fair, fare

fatal, fateful
fate, fête
feet, feat
feign, fain, fane
ferment, foment
flare, flair
flew, flue, flu
floor, flaw
flow, floe
flower, flour
for, four, fore
forebear, forbear
foregone, forgone
formally, formerly
fortunate, fortuitous
forward, foreword
fourth, forth
freeze, frieze
functional, functionary
funeral, funereal
fur, fir
further, farther
gamble, gambol
gate, gait
gentle, genteel, gentile
gild, guild
glacier, glazier
goal, gaol
gorilla, guerilla
graduate, graduand
great, grate
grill, grille
grisly, grizzly, gristly
grown, groan
guilt, gilt
hail, hale
hair, hare
hanger, hangar
heard, herd
heel, heal
here, hear
hereditary, heretical
heroin, heroine
him, hymn
historic, historical, histrionic
hoard, horde
hole, whole
horse, hoarse
human, humane
hypocritical, hypercritical
idiocy, idiosyncrasy
idle, idol, idyll
imaginary, imaginative, imaginable
immoral, amoral
imperial, imperious
implicit, explicit
inconsiderate, inconsiderable
incredible, incredulous
inculcate, inculpate
indigenous, indigent
industrious, industrial
inflammable, inflammatory
ingenious, ingenuous
inoperable, inoperative
insure, ensure, assure
intense, intensive
inveigh, inveigle
iron, ion
its, it's
jeans, genes
judicious, judicial
key, quay
layer, lair
leak, leek
least, lest
led, lead
licence, license
liniment, lineament
loan, lone
loathe, loath (loth)
lock, loch
loot, lute
lord, laud
lose, loose, loss ▷

luxurious, luxuriant
main, mane
maize, maze
male, mail
mantle, mantel
mare, mayor
mat, matt
medal, meddle
meet, meat, mete
melodious, melodic
metal, mettle
metre, meter
might, mite
miner, minor
missed, mist
moral, morale
morning, mourning
motive, motif
muscle, mussel
mute, moot
mysterious, mystical
naval, navel
navy, navvy
need, knead
neigh, nay
net, nett
nightly, knightly
noticeable, notable
nought, naught
nugget, nougat
obedience, obeisance
official, officious
operative, operable
opposite, apposite
oral, aural
ostensible, ostentatious
ought, aught
pagoda, pergola
pain, pane
pale, pail
past, passed
pastel, pastille
pathos, bathos
peace, piece
pear, pair, pare
pearl, purl
pedal, peddle
peel, peal
peer, pier
perceptive, perceptible
perpetrate, perpetuate
personal, personnel
perspective, prospective
perspicacity, perspicuity
perspicuous, perspicacious
petrify, putrefy
pistol, pistil
pitiful, piteous, pitiable
plain, plane
plaintiff, plaintive
pole, poll
politically, politicly
ponder, pander
populace, populous
popular, poplar
portent, portend
poser, poseur
potent, potential
pour, pore, paw
practical, practicable
practise, practice
prays, preys, praise
precedent, precedence
prescribe, proscribe
presents, presence
principal, principle
prize, prise
proceed, precede
prodigal, prodigious
prodigy, protégé
profit, prophet
prophecy, prophesy
prostrate, prostate
provident, providential

punctual, punctilious
quarts, quartz
queue, cue
quite, quiet
racket, racquet
raise, rays, raze
read, reed
real, reel
recent, resent
rain, rein, reign
rational, rationale
red, read
resin, rosin
respectable, respectful, respective
responsible, responsive
rest, wrest
reverend, reverent
review, revue
right, write, rite, wright
righteous, rightful
ring, wring
road, rode, rowed
roll, role
route, rout, root
rung, wrung
rye, wry
sail, sale
salutary, salubrious
seem, seam
seen, scene
seller, cellar
sensible, sensitive
sensual, sensuous, sensory
sent, scent, cent
septic, sceptic
serial, cereal
sew, so, sow
sewerage, sewage
shear, sheer
shoot, chute
sight, site, cite
signature, signatory
singing, singeing
skull, scull
slight, sleight
slow, slough
sore, soar
sort, sought
soul, sole
stair, stare
stationary, stationery
statue, stature, status, statute
stayed, staid
steak, stake
steal, steel
stimulus, stimulant
story, storey
straight, strait
sty, stye
style, stile
subside, subsidise
superficial, supercilious
surplus, surplice
swot, swat
symbol, cymbal
tacit, taciturn
tactful, tactical
tail, tale
tassel, tussle
team, teem
tear, tier, tare
temporary, temporal
their, there, they're
through, threw
throws, throes
tied, tide, tired
time, thyme
tire, tyre
to, two, too
told, tolled
tortuous, torturous
transient, transitional
triumphant, triumphal
troop, troupe ▷

uninterested, disinterested
urban, urbane
vacation, vocation
vain, vein, vane
veil, vale
verbal, verbose
virile, viral
wait, weight
waste, waist
wave, waive
weary, wary
weather, whether, wether
were, we're
wet, whet
wholly, holy, holey
whose, who's
won't, wont
wrapped, rapped, rapt
wreck, wreak
yolk, yoke
you, ewe, yew
your, you're, yore

And do you know the difference between the following?

already, all ready
altogether, all together
anyone, any one
anymore, any more
anyway, any way
everyone, every one
sometime, some time
nonetheless, none the less
forever, for ever
however, how ever

Notice the spelling *all right* for both the meaning *O.K.* and *completely correct*.

9.12 How Good is Your Spelling?

See if you can spot any errors in the spelling of the following words.

Check in your dictionary if you think you have found one.

excel
mnemonic
hypocrite
benefited
merger
tautology
appalling
resuscitate
enrolment
shriek
lackadaisical
compatible
psychic
omitted
referral
dittos
variegated
sacrilegious
embarrass
acquiesce
plausible
hypocrisy
memento
supersede
battalion
inoculate
desiccated
quarrelled
carousel
stupor
abandoned
preferred
conceited
hygiene
woollen
haemorrhage
questionnaire
anemone
irresistible

gauge
travelling
bountiful
nomenclature
picnicking
liaison
accumulate
interrogate
vigorous
disappear
remuneration
apoplexy
frolicking
mortgage
abysmal
millionaire
superintendent
abscess
forty
chrysanthemum
soliloquy
unlicensed
jodhpurs
honorary
subpoena
innocuous
trestle
temporarily
incompetent
restaurateur
pharaoh
accidentally
separate
galloped
commemorate
indefinitely
deterrent
idiosycrasy
occurrence
siege

villain
humorous
exaggerate
omelette
weird
altogether
reminiscence
parallel
tranquillity
rarefied
homogeneous
fulfilment
yacht
noticeable
calendar
procedure
jewellery
desperate
ordinary
truly
indispensable
assassin
wholly
exhilaration
proffered
facsimile
thoroughfare
accommodation
supercilious
inaccessible
unforgettable
correspondence
barbecue
preceding
wield
cemetery
instil
extraordinary
ecstasy
mischievous

leisure
relevant
independence
skilful
gauze
argument
rhythm
honourable
disappoint
transferred
marvellous
acquisition
consensus
pursue
scurrilous
innovate
ricochet
controversy
achievement
recommend
dignitary
harassment
queue
instalment
offered
preferable
murmuring
privilege
beleaguer
intriguing
notable
trespass
pavilion
miscellaneous
adjudicate
seize
threshold
infallible
phlegm
schizophrenia

10 NUMBERS

10.1 The problem with numbers is whether to write a number in figures or words. The general guides are:

Use figures when the number is part of an expression of measurement, time, currency, etc. *For example*

60km 8.30 a.m. 80c

Otherwise, in written narrative, use figures for all numbers over one hundred other than round numbers. For ease of reading it may sometimes be better to use figures for numbers less than one hundred.

Figures are generally preferred in lists.

A figure number, including those with a symbol at the front, should not begin a sentence – nor in general end one, if the number is a pure number.

10.2 Except for the tens, all numbers from twenty-one to ninety-nine have a hyphen. *For example*

seventy-three eighty-one

A hyphen is used in fractions. *For example*

one-third two and three-quarters

While a pure mathematical fraction is written with a hyphen, no hyphen is used in such expressions as the following.

one half of the population
two thirds of the estate

There is no space between the component parts in expressions such as the following.

1st 3rd 10c $5m 23° 15%

A space should be used today between each group of three digits of a number, grouped from the decimal point to the left (and right). *For example*

60 000 8 500 000

Notice the correct formulation of telephone numbers.

230 6011 68 9222 018 123 789
0055 10722 (03) 233 4567 1800 123 456

Outgoing International *(to New York, N.Y.): Dial* the International Access Code, then the country code, then the area code, then the local number, (Int.) 1 (212) 555 1234

Incoming International *(to Sydney, N.S.W.): Dial* the International Access code, then (+61 2), then the local number, 568 2444. *Note* the zero is *removed* from the area code.

In ordinal numbers the last two letters are written to the right above the numeral. In type the letters stand next to the numeral. *For example*

the 20th century	a 1st class carriage
the 21st century	the 2nd prize ribbon

Note a 12-metre pool

10.3 Useful Expressions

Observe the following correct way to write some useful expressions.

\$2 *or* \$2.00	one-fifth *or* 1/5
\$12.05	two-thirds *or* 2/3
5c	0.35
75c	51.05
27°C	27 August 1924
4.00 p.m. *or* four o'clock	27.8.24
at 1600 hours *(international time)*	Sunday, 25 July
	in 2001
11.40 a.m. *or* eleven forty	the 1990s
at 11.46 *or* 11:46	AD 33 *(*Latin *anno domini)*
at ten to two	4004 BC *(before Christ)*
the eight o'clock train	an 84-year-old husband
the eleven-thirty bus	a 600-word essay
2nd	the 20th century
10th	a 19th-century novel

10.4 Roman Numerals

Roman numerals have remained in use for certain purposes despite the general use of Arabic numbers. An explanation of Roman numerals is given below. Roman numerals are usually written in capital letters, but they may be in lower case.

The system is constructed with seven symbols standing for base numbers as in the following table.

I	(1)	**C**	(100)
V	(5)	**D**	(500)
X	(10)	**M**	(1000)
L	(50)		

The numbers 1 to 10 are written as in the following table.

I	(1)	**VI**	(6)	**i**	(1)	**vi**	(6)
II	(2)	**VII**	(7)	**ii**	(2)	**vii**	(7)
III	(3)	**VIII**	(8)	**iii**	(3)	**viii**	(8)
IV	(4)	**IX**	(9)	**iv**	(4)	**xi**	(9)
V	(5)	**X**	(10)	**v**	(5)	**x**	(10)

▷

The numbers are written according to the following rules.

(a) If a symbol is immediately followed by one of equal or less value, the values are added. *For example*

VI (6) VIII (8) XV (15) XXX (30)

(b) If a symbol is immediately followed by one of greater value, the first is subtracted from the second. *For example*

IV (4) IX (9) XL (40)

The tens are written thus:

X	(10)	**LX**	(60)
XX	(20)	**LXX**	(70)
XXX	(30)	**LXXX**	(80)
XL	(40)	**XC**	(90)
L	(50)	**C**	(100)

Further examples

XXXIV	(34)	CXVII	(117)	MCXXX	(1130)
XXXIX	(39)	CCXXI	(221)	MCDXIX	(1419)
XLI	(41)	CCCXLIX	(349)	MD	(1500)
LXXIV	(74)	CD	(400)	MDCCXC	(1790)
LXXIX	(79)	CDIX	(409)	MCMXIX	(1919)
XCII	(92)	CDXCIX	(499)	MCMLXXXIX	(1989)
XCIX	(99)	DCCIV	(704)	MCMXCVII	(1997)

It is to be noted that the symbols **I**, **X** and **C** are used in front of a symbol of greater value to subtract their appropriate value rather than having a long string of the same symbols for addition.

In Roman numbers no ordinal indication appears: the XIV Commonwealth Games, the XXVII Olympiad, Queen Elizabeth II.

11 PUNCTUATION

As will have been appreciated, the hyphen, the apostrophe and the full stop are intimately related to spelling as a part of written language. It will be to the reader's advantage if a few words of advice are given concerning other punctuation marks as they too are virtually an intimate part of a sentence. And a further few words will be added in the case of the functions already described.

The purpose of punctuation is to make the reading as clear as possible. It is to be understood however that these notes are by no means an exhaustive treatment, but they will stand the reader in good stead.

We are in no way helped by the failure of dictionaries to define the true nature of punctuation marks. Dictionary definitions tell of the relative *force* of punctuation marks in breaking the sentence. Rather it is a question of punctuation marks' having as their function the forming of a whole. From this viewpoint, an attempt is made here to explain their use. The principles outlined in what follows are in keeping with the most common Australian practice, which agrees fairly generally with what is the most common practice in Britain, indeed for the most part in America, and in other English-speaking countries.

Full Stop

The main function of the full stop is to denote the end of a sentence unless a question mark or an exclamation mark is to stand there. In direct speech, the closing inverted commas will follow.

At the end of a polite request, a full stop is used. Despite the form of a request such as the following, the request is not a question.

"Would you pass me the salt please."

No full stop is used in a title or a heading.

In cases where strict usage calls for a full stop immediately after another full stop, a question mark or an exclamation mark, the seemingly necessary full stop is omitted.

As explained in *Section 8*, a full stop is also used after shortened forms not ending with the last letter of the abbreviated word.

Apostrophe

The use of the apostrophe is dealt with fully in *Section 5*.

Hyphen

A hyphen has other functions than that of joining two words in a compound or linking word breaks at the end of a line *(see Section 7)*.

A hyphen is used to indicate a stutter: W-w-what? and to show the spelling of a word: c-o-l-o-u-r. It is also used with an inclusive function: 1939-1945, August-September.

Question Mark

A question mark stands at the end of a direct question. It is also used at the end of a rhetorical question, one to which no answer is expected. *For example*

"Where have they gone?'' she asked.
"They actually did that?"
Where is education headed?
"Do you take me for a fool?"

Note carefully the treatment of the question mark in the following situations.

His question was: "Why should we?"
Did he say: "I shall return"?
Were her actual words: "Who was present?"
Did she exclaim: "What bad luck!''?

A question mark is also used to indicate doubt.

Richard Blassing (1581? – 1648)

Exclamation Mark

An exclamation mark is used at the end of an exclamatory outcry or emphatic comment. *For example*

"Help!"
"Are we relieved!"
"I don't believe it!"
"What luck!"
That it should have come to this!

An exclamation mark is also used after a set exclamation or an interjection. *For example*

Happy birthday!
Your health!
Hear, hear!
Heaven forbid!
Dear me!

Comma

A comma is used in English as an aid to the reading of a sentence. Its purpose is to make the reading easier by its being clearer. The comma serves as an indicator to pause either when the sentence is long so that the reader will not be confused, or when it is necessary to take in some thought before the reader proceeds. This will very often be the case as we proceed from one clause to the next. But remember that too many commas jar, too few confuse.

An introductory word or words of transition *(however, moreover, furthermore,* etc.), names of address, interjections, words indicating hesitation, are followed by a comma. Any of these words used within a clause may well be marked off with commas if there is need for a pause.

A comma is mostly used before and after an adverbial clause unless the clause is very short. An adjectival clause that defines rather than describes should not be set off with a comma or commas. The same applies to defining words or phrases or even other clauses. Defining signifies an essential modification, which if omitted would change the meaning or leave the sentence without meaning.

My son Robert, who is only sixteen, won the trophy.
The trophy was again awarded to the boy who won it last year.

Be careful not to separate a noun or pronoun subject by only one comma from its verb. The same applies to the verb and its object. Be careful also not to separate the subordinating conjunction *that* by only one comma from its clause because of an intervening clause.

To keep things simple, just take the advice to use a comma or commas in order to assist those reading what you have written. Just examine the following sentences and see the clarity stemming from the use of the commas.

Whatever he does, has my blessing.
To appreciate his goodness, is reward enough.
He recognised the woman who had entered the room,
and gasped.
In 1975, 1400 students were in attendance.
On the hill above, a great temple stood.
To Bill, Jones was a peculiar fellow.

Note the obligatory use of the comma at the end of direct speech when no other punctuation mark stands or at a sentence break. The comma is incorporated in the speech.

"We are leaving on Tuesday," he said.
"Don't shoot!" he cried.
"What is that?" she asked.
"This example," said the judge, "should not be followed."

Notice however where the comma stands with the dash or ellipsis points of incomplete speech.

"If only I were younger –", he sighed.

Some uses of the comma are formal devices:

(a) The addressing of people by name.

"Bob, come here."
"I want you, Bob, to assist."

(b) In such instances as when a day of the week is followed by a precise date.

Wednesday, 27 August

(c) In a series to separate the items except in the case where the word *and* is used between the last two.

(d) To separate co-ordinate adjectives (adjectives of equal descriptive significance) before a noun.

a generous, affectionate man
a big black dog

Note The word *and* can be placed between co-ordinate adjectives.

(e) Sometimes a comma (rather than a colon) is used to introduce direct speech or a quotation if the speech consists of only one sentence.

Inverted Commas

Quotation marks (double inverted commas) are used to indicate direct speech or a quotation.

Direct speech or a quotation is introduced by a colon.

She exclaimed: "I am terribly afraid!"

Notice that the opening commas are *upside down* and that the punctuation mark of the actual speech is placed inside the closing inverted commas.

"I was terribly afraid," she said.

If the direct speech does not close the sentence, a comma is used inside the inverted commas instead of what would otherwise have been a full stop.

If the speech or quotation extends over more than one paragraph, quotation marks are placed at the beginning of each paragraph, but the closing marks are placed only at the end of the last paragraph.

A broken sentence is punctuated as in the following example.

"At first," he said, "I was terribly afraid."

A comma (rather than a colon) is usually used to introduce direct speech or a quotation if short.

As Julian wrote, "To have tried is reward enough."
According to Churchill, "that's not the plan."

Whether a capital letter is used immediately after the comma or not depends much upon the nature of the situation.

Inverted commas are also used to *draw attention* to some word or phrase in the sentence or to enclose slang and technical terms. If this word or phrase is quoted from conversation or writing, double inverted commas will be used. If not, a set of single inverted commas is used.

> His concept of the 'ideal life' differed radically from mine.
> She said that the concert was "a bit in the balance".

Notice the position of the full stop in the latter example. The full stop belongs to the whole sentence not just to the section in inverted commas. The section in inverted commas is a quotation from direct speech.

The continuing of the use of the inverted commas is necessary in further reference only if there is a special point to it. The learner is advised to tread cautiously here. Carefully observe usage in good writing.

The use of single inverted commas is also useful for marking off a quotation within direct speech.

> "I heard the gunman say: 'I want the women'," the student reported.
> "I've never had to tell him, 'Jimmy, do your homework'," she said.
> "People warned me, 'Don't say anything, don't talk to anyone'," she cried.

If in such circumstances the quotation continues into a second paragraph, there is need to begin the paragraph with both double inverted commas and a single inverted comma.

Remember that inverted commas *(see Section 6.7c)* are used when reference is made to the chapters of books, magazines etc., titles of articles, short poems and songs, radio and television programmes.

For the dialogue of a play or an interview, quotation marks are not used. When lines of poetry are quoted and set off separately, no inverted commas should be used. Inverted commas are not used for the names of buildings or for music pieces bearing a technical title. At times however, particularly in letter writing, the name of a house is written with inverted commas.

Summary Double inverted commas are used for quoted speech or writing and also to refer to certain literary titles and headings. Single inverted commas are used to draw attention to a word or words and to mark off a quotation within direct speech.

Some authorities avoid completely the use of single inverted commas except for the case of quotation within quotation. Some newspapers reserve single inverted commas for use in headings. The not infrequent use of single inverted commas for direct speech is a practice best not imitated.

It is to be noted that (other than in direct speech) American practice in the placing of full stops and commas inside closing inverted commas differs from general practice elsewhere.

Colon

The colon is used to introduce direct speech or a quotation.

> The captain said: "We sail on the tide."
> The quotation begins: "Until the end of the century ..."

Provided that there is no grammatical break in the sentence, a colon is also used mid-sentence to indicate a listing, to introduce examples, to present the main theme, to define a word or situation, to illustrate, to explain, enlarge or summarise, to mark an antithesis. It also serves to indicate a ratio (4:1) and it is used in a biblical reference (John 3:16) with volume and page numbers (2:19-21), and sometimes in time expressions (5:15).

Semicolon

A semicolon is used when another aspect of the statement just made is to be presented. A semicolon is also used after each item in a complex series, especially one containing elements with commas.

Dash

A dash can serve to present an explanation or an antithesis or to *gather up* preceding elements in order to make a general conclusion. If the explanation is made in the middle of a sentence, a set of dashes will enclose the explanation. A set of dashes can help to clarify an involved sentence. A dash is also used to denote an abrupt change or interrupted speech. Dashes also indicate the omission of letters or words, especially in guessing competitions. In this case, the dashes sit on the base line. *For example*

> O L _ M P _ C   G A _ E _ *(Olympic Games)*

Brackets

Brackets *(round)*, known as parentheses, are used to enclose words that have an explanatory function, perhaps acting as a reminder or serving to translate a phrase from another tongue.

Square brackets should be used to enclose insertions in the text from someone other than the author and also to indicate other interpolations.

Ellipsis Points

Ellipsis points *(three dots ...)* are used to denote an omission of some words or a large section from a quoted passage. They are also used to indicate faltering speech, perhaps the consequence of great excitement or rapture, of diffidence or reluctance.

Diaeresis

A diaeresis is a pronunciation aid. It is a mark (*two dots*) placed over a vowel *(*as in *naïve)* indicating that it is sounded separately.

Foreign Accents

In the spelling of quite a number of words borrowed from a foreign language (especially French), the use of the accent is still preferred (*résumé*, *château*, etc.); in others its use is optional (*rôle*, *façade*, *élite*, etc.). Dictionaries are hopelessly at odds with each other on this point *(see Section 9.6)*.

Italics (Underlining in Writing)

To make special reference to a word or phrase, sparing use may be made of underlining (in writing or typing) or of italics (in print), this as an alternative to the use of single inverted commas. This applies in particular to a word or words cited as such (the letter *k*, the word *apartheid*, the term *blue zone*, etc.). In further references to the expression, there may well be no need to continue the use of the italics or the underlining.

Italics (*or* underlining) are also used to indicate a foreign word or expression that has not yet been fully assimilated into English.

See Section 6.7 for the use of italics with certain titles.

Oblique

Also known as a diagonal, slash or solidus, an oblique is used to indicate alternatives, in certain standard abbreviations, to denote a fraction and to express the concept *per*. *For example*

yes/no   a/c   C/ – $^2/_5$ 80km/h $125/m

Special Note

In your reading of books, magazines and newspapers, you will come upon many departures from the punctuation procedures defined in the above notes. Some of these differences may be acceptable, the majority not. Some institutions have their own style guide or follow that of some other authority. You are also warned that American practice varies from what is best practice in the British Commonwealth. Again the admonition is given that if you are guided by the principles outlined in *Spelling English* no one can fault your punctuation.

There are of course technical details that lie beyond the scope of these basic guides. Furthermore, a writer can at times get into a complicated situation not specifically analysed in the instructions given. Journalists in their intermixing of direct and indirect speech are frequently caught in this web. The advice is not to complicate your sentences.

12 TABLE OF IRREGULAR VERBS

In some cases where alternative forms exist, use may be governed by circumstance, literary context, poetry, particular meaning, striving for archaic flavour, etc.

Infinitive	Past tense	Past participle	Present tense
arise	arose	arisen	arises
awake	awoke	awoken	awakes
be	was	been	is
bear	bore	borne *or* born	bears
beat	beat	beaten	beats
become	became	become	becomes
begin	began	begun	begins
behold	beheld	beheld	beholds
bend	bent	bent	bends
beseech	besought *or* beseeched	besought *or* beseeched	beseeches
bid	bade *or* bid	bid *or* bidden	bids
bind	bound	bound	binds
bite	bit	bitten	bites
bleed	bled	bled	bleeds
blow	blew	blown	blows
break	broke	broken	breaks
breed	bred	bred	breeds
bring	brought	brought	brings
build	built	built	builds
burn	burnt *or* burned	burnt *or* burned	burns
burst	burst	burst	bursts
buy	bought	bought	buys
cast	cast	cast	casts
catch	caught	caught	catches
choose	chose	chosen	chooses
cleave *(split)*	clove *or* cleft	cloven *or* cleft	cleaves
cleave *(adhere)*	cleaved *or* clave	cleaved	cleaves
cling	clung	clung	clings
clothe	clothed *or* clad	clothed *or* clad	clothes
come	came	come	comes
cost	cost	cost	costs
creep	crept	crept	creeps
crow	crowed *or* crew	crowed	crows
cut	cut	cut	cuts
deal	dealt	dealt	deals

Infinitive	**Past tense**	**Past participle**	**Present tense**
dig	dug	dug	digs
do	did	done	does
draw	drew	drawn	draws
dream	dreamt *or* dreamed	dreamt *or* dreamed	dreams
drink	drank	drunk	drinks
drive	drove	driven	drives
dwell	dwelt	dwelt	dwells
eat	ate	eaten	eats
fall	fell	fallen	falls
feed	fed	fed	feeds
feel	felt	felt	feels
fight	fought	fought	fights
find	found	found	finds
flee	fled	fled	flees
fling	flung	flung	flings
fly	flew	flown	flies
forbear	forbore	forborne	forbears
forbid	forbade *or* forbad	forbidden	forbids
forget	forgot	forgotten	forgets
forgive	forgave	forgiven	forgives
forsake	forsook	forsaken	forsakes
freeze	froze	frozen	freezes
get	got	got	gets
give	gave	given	gives
go	went	gone	goes
grind	ground	ground	grinds
grow	grew	grown	grows
hang *(suspend)*	hung	hung	hangs
have	had	had	has
hear	heard	heard	hears
hew	hewed	hewn *or* hewed	hews
hide	hid	hidden	hides
hit	hit	hit	hits
hold	held	held	holds
hurt	hurt	hurt	hurts
keep	kept	kept	keeps
kneel	knelt	knelt	kneels
knit	knitted *or* knit	knitted *or* knit	knits
know	knew	known	knows
lay	laid	laid	lays

▷

Infinitive	Past tense	Past participle	Present tense
lead	led	led	leads
lean	leant *or* leaned	leant *or* leaned	leans
leap	leapt *or* leaped	leapt *or* leaped	leaps
learn	learnt *or* learned	learnt *or* learned	learns
leave	left	left	leaves
lend	lent	lent	lends
let	let	let	lets
lie (*recline*)	lay	lain	lies
light	lit *or* lighted	lit *or* lighted	lights
lose	lost	lost	loses
make	made	made	makes
mean	meant	meant	means
meet	met	met	meets
mow	mowed	mowed *or* mown	mows
pay	paid	paid	pays
prove	proved	proved *or* proven	proves
put	put	put	puts
quit	quitted *or* quit	quitted *or* quit	quits
read	read	read	reads
rend	rent	rent	rends
rid	ridded	rid	rids
ride	rode	ridden	rides
ring	rang	rung	rings
rise	rose	risen	rises
run	ran	run	runs
saw	sawed	sawn *or* sawed	saws
say	said	said	says
see	saw	seen	sees
seek	sought	sought	seeks
sell	sold	sold	sells
send	sent	sent	sends
set	set	set	sets
sew	sewed	sewn *or* sewed	sews
shake	shook	shaken	shakes
shear	sheared *or* shore	shorn *or* sheared	shears
shed	shed	shed	sheds
shine	shone	shone	shines
shoe	shod	shod	shoes

Infinitive	Past tense	Past participle	Present tense
shoot	shot	shot	shoots
show	showed	shown *or* showed	shows
shrink	shrank	shrunk *or* shrunken	shrinks
shut	shut	shut	shuts
sing	sang	sung	sings
sink	sank	sunk	sinks
sit	sat	sat	sits
slay	slew	slain	slays
sleep	slept	slept	sleeps
slide	slid	slid	slides
sling	slung	slung	slings
slink	slunk	slunk	slinks
slit	slit	slit	slits
smell	smelt *or* smelled	smelt *or* smelled	smells
smite	smote	smitten	smites
sow	sowed	sown *or* sowed	sows
speak	spoke	spoken	speaks
speed	speeded *or* sped	speeded *or* sped	speeds
spell	spelt *or* spelled	spelt *or* spelled	spells
spend	spent	spent	spends
spill	spilt *or* spilled	spilt *or* spilled	spills
spin	spun	spun	spins
spit	spat	spat	spits
split	split	split	splits
spoil	spoilt *or* spoiled	spoilt *or* spoiled	spoils
spread	spread	spread	spreads
spring	sprang	sprung	springs
stand	stood	stood	stands
steal	stole	stolen	steals
stick	stuck	stuck	sticks
sting	stung	stung	stings
stink	stank	stunk	stinks
strew	strewed	strewn *or* strewed	strews
stride	strode	stridden	strides
strike	struck	struck	strikes
string	strung	strung	strings
strive	strove	striven	strives

▷

Infinitive	Past tense	Past participle	Present tense
swear	swore	sworn	swears
sweep	swept	swept	sweeps
swell	swelled	swollen *or* swelled	swells
swim	swam	swum	swims
swing	swung	swung	swings
take	took	taken	takes
teach	taught	taught	teaches
tear	tore	torn	tears
tell	told	told	tells
think	thought	thought	thinks
thrive	thrived *or* throve	thrived *or* thriven	thrives
throw	threw	thrown	throws
thrust	thrust	thrust	thrusts
tread	trod	trodden *or* trod	treads
wake	woke *or* waked	waked, woken *or* woke	wakes
wear	wore	worn	wears
weave	wove	woven	weaves
weep	wept	wept	weeps
wet	wet *or* wetted	wet *or* wetted	wets
win	won	won	wins
wind	wound	wound	winds
work	worked *or* wrought	worked *or* wrought	works
wring	wrung	wrung	wrings
write	wrote	written	writes

Archaic verbal forms no longer in ordinary use are not included in the above lists. Some older past participle forms of these verbs and of others now fully regular have survived in adjectival use. *For example*

on bended knee
one's bounden duty
a drunken person
ill-gotten gains
a cart laden with grain
sunken cheeks
stricken with leprosy
vellum-wove paper
molten lead
his pent-up rage

INDEX

1 GENERAL SPELLING *Page*

2 PREFIXES

3 SUFFIXES *Page*

4 PLURAL OF NOUNS

5 USE OF THE APOSTROPHE

6 CAPITAL LETTERS

7 USE OF THE HYPHEN

8 SHORTENED FORMS

9 SPELLING WATCHPOINTS

10 NUMBERS

11 PUNCTUATION

The Deaf Manual Alphabet

(Courtesy of the Deaf Society of New South Wales)

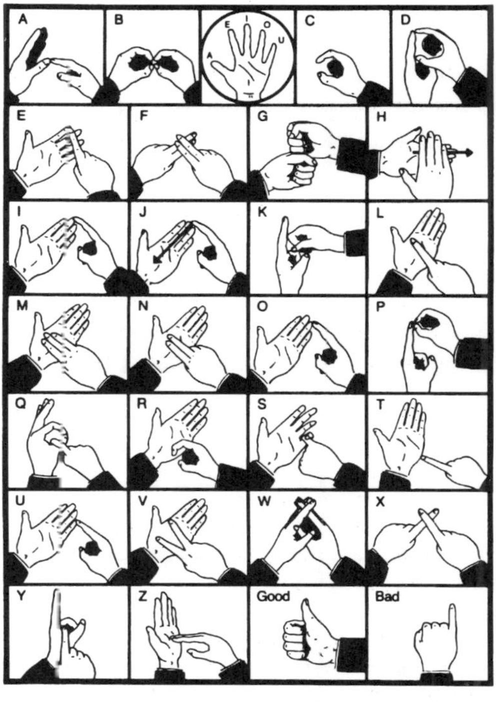

GLOSSARY

Noun the name of a person, place or thing
Pronoun a word acting as a substitute for a noun
Verb the *doing* or *being* or *having* word in each clause
Adjective a word that describes a noun or pronoun
Adverb a word that usually modifies a verb
Preposition a word that shows the relationship between things
Conjunction a word used for joining words, phrases and clauses
Interjection an exclamatory word expressing emotion

Abbreviation a shortened form using the front part of a word
Assimilation the process of absorption of a word in a language
Borrowed word a word taken over from a foreign language
Comparative degree expressing a higher degree of a quality
Compound word a word composed of two base words
Consonant a speech sound that is obstructed in its production by complete or partial closure of the vocal organs
Contraction a shortened form using parts of a word
Definite article the word *the*
Derivative a word that is formed from another word
Direct speech the actual words spoken
Indefinite article the words *a* or *an*
Irregular verb a verb that does not follow the regular pattern in changing its form
Juxtaposition placement side by side
Latin the former language of the Romans
Literary term an expression used in referring to literature
Monosyllable a word of one syllable
Past participle a verb form used to construct the perfect tense and as an adjective
Plural denoting more than one
Polysyllable a word of more than one syllable
Possessive the ownership form of a noun or pronoun
Predicative adjective an adjective used not in front of its noun
Prefix a word element added to the beginning of a word
Present participle a verb form in *-ing*
Punctuation mark a mark used to assist the understanding for the reader *(see Section 11)*
Singular denoting only one
Sound symbol a letter or letters used to indicate a sound
Suffix a letter or syllable added to the end of a word
Superlative degree expressing the highest degree of a quality
Syllable a segment of a word containing one vowel sound with or without consonants
Tense the form of the verb indicating the time of the action
Vowel one of the more open sounds used in speaking, since the air stream is not obstructed (regarded as the opposite of a consonant)